ANSWERING GOD'S CALL TO COVENANT

LUMEN CHRISTI
CATHOLIC FORMATION

11300 N. St. James Lane
Mequon, WI 53092

ANSWERING GOD'S CALL TO COVENANT

WHICH WAY TO THE REST OF YOUR LIFE?

BY JERRY WINDLEY-DAOUST

SAINT MARY'S PRESS®

Genuine recycled paper with 10% post-consumer waste. 5103900

The publishing team included Steven McGlaun, development editor; Lorraine Kilmartin, reviewer; Mary Koehler, permissions editor; prepress and manufacturing coordinated by the prepublication and production services departments of Saint Mary's Press.

Some in-text and cover background images are from Aridi Computer Graphics, Inc., copyright © 1993–1995, and Golden Era Studios, copyright © 2000.

Printed in the United States of America

Printing: 9 8 7 6 5 4 3 2 1

Year: 2013 12 11 10 09 08 07 06 05

ISBN 0-88489-883-0

Library of Congress Cataloging-in-Publication Data
Windley-Daoust, Jerry.
    Answering God's call to covenant : which way to the rest of your life? / written by Jerry Windley-Daoust ; edited by Steven C. McGlaun.
        p. cm.
    ISBN 0-88489-883-0 (pbk.)
    1. Catholic youth—Religious life. 2. Covenants—Religious aspects—Catholic Church. I. McGlaun, Steven C. II. Title.
BX2355.W56 2005
248.8'3—dc22
                                                                                2005003135

The basic concept for this book was developed by Clare vanBrandwijk, Stephan Nagel, Shirley Kelter, and Jerry Windley-Daoust. The methodology is based on the shared Christian praxis pedagogy developed by Thomas Groome as described in his book *Sharing Faith: A Comprehensive Approach to Religious Education and Pastoral Ministry.* Clare vanBrandwijk worked on another project for Saint Mary's Press; the general outline of this book, along with certain thoughts and ideas, were inspired by her work. Several passages in this book, and many of the secondary sources, are from the manuscript she wrote. Cesar Abella, Jaime Johnson, Alison Keohane, Nathan Lattyak, Michele Potofsky, Christina Rivera, and Marcu Whitlock spent countless hours over several years as student consultants for the project that preceded this book; their thoughtful critiques and contributions were invaluable in the development of the present book.

CONTENTS

JOURNEYING INTO YOUNG ADULTHOOD

 WOULD YOU TELL ME, PLEASE, WHICH WAY I OUGHT TO GO FROM HERE?"

"THAT DEPENDS A GOOD DEAL ON WHERE YOU WANT TO GET TO," SAID THE CAT.

"I DON'T MUCH CARE WHERE——" SAID ALICE.

"THEN IT DOESN'T MATTER WHICH WAY YOU GO," SAID THE CAT.

(Lewis Carroll, *Alice's Adventures in Wonderland*)

Your high school years are drawing to a close, and young adulthood lies just around the corner. Sometime in the next few years, you will probably find yourself standing at a crossroads like Alice, wondering, "Which way do I go now?" The crossroads of young adulthood often takes the form of life-shaping questions, some of them more obvious than others:

- What career should I pursue?
- What values do I need to hold fast to, and what values can I place a lesser priority upon?
- Where is this romantic relationship going?
- How do I take charge of my life?
- What does my faith look like, and what role will it play in my life?

As the Cat pointed out to Alice, your answer to these crossroads questions will depend on where you want to go in life.

The Call to Covenant

This book was written to help you think about the question "Where do I want to go in life?" before you encounter the crossroads of young adulthood. Poor Alice could ask only a smart-aleck cat for direction; this book proposes that you consult a wiser guide.

More than three thousand years ago, God called the Israelite people to set out on a journey toward a richer, happier life. That journey was not without uncertainty or danger, but the people had an unfailing guide: "The LORD went in front of them in a pillar of cloud by day, to lead them along the way, and in a pillar of fire by night, to give them light, so that they might travel by day and by night" (Exodus 13:21). As the people began their journey, God made a Covenant with them: God promised always to guide and protect them if they would promise always to follow God.

As you begin the journey into adulthood, God calls you to a rich and happy life, too. Like the Israelites, you are called to enter a covenant with him (see *Catechism of the Catholic Church,* no. 357): God will light the way to a happy life if you choose to follow him.

About This Book

This book sets out seven crossroads questions that you will probably encounter in the next five years, and it invites you to consider your response in light of God's call to covenant:

1. HOW WILL I RESPOND TO CHANGE?
2. WHO DO I WANT TO BE?
3. HOW WILL I FIND HAPPINESS?
4. HOW WILL I FIND LOVE AND FRIENDSHIP?
5. WHAT WILL I TAKE WITH ME?
6. WHAT PATH WILL I CHOOSE?
7. WHICH WAY TO THE REST OF MY LIFE?

Such foundational questions may seem less pressing when you are faced with other more immediate and practical concerns. But the questions are important crossroads questions because the way you answer them will influence the way you respond to the many practical questions of young adulthood—and more important, where you end up as an adult.

Each of the first six chapters of this book follows a similar three-part format:

THE QUESTION. The first part of each chapter briefly explores the crossroads, or focus, question of the chapter. The first part of the chapter also provides some space for thinking about how you might answer the question now, in light of your current thought and experience.

THE COVENANT. This section looks at how Christian faith answers the chapter focus question in light of the Covenant that God established with the Israelites and renewed through Jesus Christ. That Covenant (capital C) forms the basis for the personal covenant (lowercase c) to which God calls you.

YOUR RESPONSE. Once you have considered how your faith responds to the chapter focus question, you are invited to consider prayerfully how you want to live your response to the question as a young adult.

Throughout each chapter, a handful of reflection questions will invite you to explore the chapter focus question from different angles. The purpose of these reflection questions is not to test your knowledge of the chapter content; rather, they are meant to give you time to really think about where you want to go in life. Think of your responses to these questions as a kind of road map for your journey into young adulthood.

Record your responses to these questions, along with any other thoughts or reflections you might have, in a notebook or journal. (Or, if you prefer, you could make an audio or video recording of your responses for later reference.) Space is provided in this book for your initial response or notes. It is important that you record your responses to the reflection questions because in the last chapter, you will review those responses to create a covenant statement, a kind of personal mission statement made in light of the Covenant. The purpose of that statement is to make a commitment to God and yourself about the basic direction you want to take in life; as you face the changes and challenges of the next few years, that covenant statement can serve as a resource.

↳ LIVING THE QUESTIONS

Finally, a word of caution: it would be a mistake to imagine that you can or should answer the questions in this book completely and finally. The German poet Rainer Maria Rilke offers appropriate advice:

> BE PATIENT TOWARDS ALL THAT IS UNSOLVED IN YOUR HEART AND TRY TO LOVE THE QUESTIONS THEMSELVES LIKE LOCKED ROOMS. . . . DO NOT SEEK THE ANSWERS THAT CANNOT BE GIVEN YOU BECAUSE YOU WOULD NOT BE ABLE TO LIVE THEM. AND THE POINT IS, TO LIVE EVERYTHING.
>
> *L*IVE THE QUESTIONS NOW, PERHAPS YOU WILL THEN GRADUALLY, WITHOUT NOTICING IT, LIVE ALONG SOME DISTANT DAY INTO THE ANSWER.

(*Letters to a Young Poet,* p. 35)

To "live the questions" is not to avoid them or to treat them as unanswerable. Rather, to live the questions is to remain hopeful that, as you make your way through life by the light of God, your responses will become ever deeper and wiser.

With that in mind, let's begin living the questions and start on the journey through the countless possibilities before you. Waiting on the other side is your unique covenant with God.

How Will I Respond to Change?

↳ The Question

On the Threshold of Life

I was filled with melancholy the other day. I had spent such a wonderful night camping with my friends. Yet it hit me when I was talking to one of my friends. There we were on the swing looking at an impressive sunrise, and I wondered, "Who knows how many more times I will see him?" College will begin pretty soon and I will meet new people and my relationship with him will suspend. I will change, he will change, and each time we get together again we will be more distant. It seems as if I will be living in two different worlds—the friends I have in college will have no idea of my life at home or vice versa. I will be a person living within many realms, trying to maintain relationships with people so far away, being separated, coming back, changing. (Clémence Sullivan)

I thought about what I really wanted. . . . One part of me wanted to have a good, normal job, and a good education, and the other wanted me to do something outrageously fun for my life, and to hell with money and education and stability. (Jason Longo, in *Our Boys Speak*, p. 116)

My time is up here. Four years of my life have been filled with joy, security, and self-confidence. But now all I see is uncertainty. A whole new world is waiting for me, but with no direction it seems. My path is unclear, and I am afraid I will choose the wrong road. The time is approaching when I will have to depend more and more on myself—and I'm unsure how to handle this. Do I worry? Should I be nervous? Who will help me? (C. C., in *Turn Into the Wind*, p. 80)

Do any of these voices sound familiar? Like you, these young people are coming to the end of their high school years. They're starting to think about life after high school, and those thoughts bring on a wide range of feelings: excitement about the freedom and potential of young-adult life, worry about new and unknown challenges, sadness or even grief at saying good-bye to friends and a comfortably familiar way of life.

All these feelings are normal for people whose lives are undergoing great change—and no doubt, leaving your teenage years and entering young adulthood involves great change. Just think about everything the young people quoted above will probably experience in the five years following their high school graduation:

- saying goodbye to old friends and making new ones
- leaving their family homes to live on their own
- choosing a career path and getting a job
- managing their own finances
- assuming the rights and responsibilities that come with legal adulthood
- entering into romantic relationships

In short, these young people are about to enter one of the most change-filled periods of their lives. How will *you* respond to the changes of this upcoming period?

PAUSE TO REFLECT

A. Start by thinking of the big changes and transitions you have already experienced in your life—for example, a move to another school or city, the death of a friend, the start of a new job, or the beginning of a new relationship. The way you handled these transitions offers some clues about how you might deal with the transition into young adulthood. Do you tend to embrace change, resist it, or a little of both? What do you think you handled well about these transitions, and what would you do differently now if you could do them over?

B. Make a list of the changes you expect to encounter in the next five years or so (you can use the list above for ideas). After each change, write a little about how the change makes you feel (sad? excited? indifferent?) and why.

WHERE DO I GO FROM HERE

No one can tell you exactly what to expect on the journey into young adulthood. Fortunately, though, others who have been through major life changes can help you prepare.

THREE STAGES OF CHANGE

William Bridges, author of the book *Transitions: Making Sense of Life's Changes,* believes that major life transitions come in three stages.

- **Endings.** All changes begin with endings; an old chapter of life must come to a close before a new chapter of life can begin. Endings involve letting go of an old way of life—the social roles (for example, student, teammate, baby-sitter) and routines (studying, doing family chores, hanging out with high school friends) that fill our days. And to the extent that we define ourselves according to our daily activities and social relationships, ending these things also means letting go of our old identity, our sense of who we are.

- **The desert.** After their old life has ended, but before they are totally adjusted to their new life, many people experience a time of emptiness and loneliness—maybe even a sense of being a little lost. They've left familiar routines and roles behind but haven't really established new ones yet. The Christian saints and mystics compared this in-between place to a desert. Most people who find themselves in the empty, lonely space of the desert want nothing more than to get out—the sooner, the better! But in the Christian tradition, the emptiness of the desert is often where people encounter God and undergo great transformation.

- **Beginnings.** On the outside, beginning a new way of life is about adjusting to new social roles (such as new friends, a different relationship with parents) and new routines (doing your own laundry and grocery shopping, for instance). On a deeper level, beginning a new way of life means coming to a new understanding of who we are.

This pattern of change applies equally well to the transitions we welcome (like going to college) and to those we resist (like the end of a relationship). Whether we view the changes in our life as "good" or "bad," a key question is how to deal with those changes in a healthy, life-giving way. A lot of people try to control change to reach a good end, which makes sense. If we have to get a job, for example, we may as well choose the best one available. But sooner or later everyone encounters changes they can't control. What then?

We may not always be able to control life's changes. But we can control how we *respond* to those changes.

TWO STORIES FROM THE DESERT

Two biblical stories offer wisdom for anyone facing transition and change. The first story describes the Israelites' transition from slavery to freedom; the second describes Jesus's transition from private life to public ministry.

ISRAEL IN THE DESERT

The story of the Exodus opens with the Israelites living in Egypt as slaves. They cry out to God for an end to this way of life; God hears their plea and chooses Moses and Aaron to lead them to a new life in a better land, the Promised Land. God frees the Israelites by leading them safely through the waters of the sea. They are overjoyed to see their old way of life come to an end—at least, at first they are.

Before they can reach the Promised Land, though, they must pass through the desert. God travels with them, going before them in a pillar of cloud by day and a pillar of fire by night (see Exodus 13:21). Along the way, God claims them as his people and calls them to enter a sacred Covenant with him:

> "You have seen what I did to the Egyptians, and how I bore you on eagles' wings and brought you to myself. Now therefore, if you obey my voice and keep my covenant, you shall be my treasured posses-sion out of all the peoples. Indeed, the whole earth is mine, but you shall be for me a priestly kingdom and a holy nation." (19:4–6)

"Everything that the LORD has spoken we will do," the people respond (19:8). In the ancient world, a covenant was a solemn, binding agreement between two persons or groups. The Ten Commandments enumerated the basic obligations of the Covenant—love of God and neighbor.

Given the promise of God's constant care, it should have been easy for the Israelites to leave the desert to begin their new life in the Promised Land—but it wasn't. Again and again, they failed to trust God. First, they didn't trust God to feed them in the desert; they even longed for their old life in Egypt, where there was plenty of food to eat (see Exodus 16:3; Numbers 11:4–6). Then, they thought Moses and God had abandoned them, and they built a golden calf to worship instead of God (see Exodus 32:1–6). Finally, they wouldn't enter the Promised Land because they didn't trust that God would help them overcome the enemies who blocked their way. Again they longed for their old way of life: "Would it not be better for us to go back to Egypt?" (Numbers 14:3). Again and again, God renewed his Covenant with the people despite their lack of trust.

The Israelites' story is a very human one. It's the way most of us handle life's transitions—bumpily, with fits and starts and moments of doubt. When this is our experience, it's important to remember that God never abandoned the Israelites, even when they abandoned God.

JESUS IN THE DESERT

The story of Jesus's transition from his old, private life as a carpenter to his new life of public ministry bears some resemblance to Israel's story. Like Israel, Jesus left his old life by passing through water when his cousin John baptized him. The Spirit led Jesus, like Israel, into the desert. But look at how he responded to this time in the desert differently than did Israel:

🔹 Like Israel, Jesus was hungry in the desert. But when Jesus was tempted to turn a stone into bread, he responded, "It is written,

'One does not live by bread alone,
but by every word that comes from the mouth of God'"

(Matthew 4:4)

🔹 When the Israelites lost their trust in God, they made a golden calf to worship instead. But when Jesus was tempted to worship Satan in exchange for worldly power, Jesus answered, "It is written,

'Worship the Lord your God,
and serve only him.'"

(Matthew 4:10)

Israel hesitated to enter the Promised Land because the people didn't trust that the Lord would keep them safe. But when Jesus was tempted to test the Father's care for him, Jesus responded, "It is said, 'Do not put the Lord your God to the test'" (Luke 4:12).

All of Jesus's responses have a common element: he trusted the Father to carry him safely through the desert. God will carry us safely through the desert as well, if we have the same kind of trust Jesus had.

YOU IN THE DESERT

Just as Israel and Jesus had to go through the desert to get to a better life beyond, you too will probably find yourself in the stillness, silence, and emptiness of the desert at some point in the next few years. But as the stories of Israel and Jesus affirm, the desert isn't necessarily something to be feared. It was in passing through the desert that the Israelites rediscovered a new identity as God's Chosen People, and it was in the desert that Jesus's identity as the Son of God was revealed (see Matthew 3:17, 4:3). It is the same way with each of us during times of transition and change. When our days are stripped bare of the roles and routines that normally distract us, the resulting emptiness creates more space for God's transforming presence to enter our lives.

Instead of being afraid of transitions, we can ask: "How is God present in this time? What kind of new life and identity might God call me to during this time of change?"

Those who follow Christ can enter any time of transition and change with confidence, because he has already gone through the greatest transition of all—the passage from death to new life. And by virtue of our baptism, we have already traveled through the desert of the Passion with him.

By participating in Jesus's death and Resurrection through Baptism, we died to our old selves and were reborn into a new identity, one in which we became God's "adopted" children. We can hear the words that God spoke to Israel as if they are spoken to us: "You shall be my treasured possession."

Trusting that Jesus will carry us safely through the desert of change doesn't mean we won't falter, like Israel. Nor does it mean the way will be easy. Jesus trusted his Father completely yet experienced fear (see Mark 14:32–36) and even a sense of abandonment (see Mark 15:34). Rather, trusting Christ means remembering that no matter what life throws at us, God's love has already triumphed. If we've already been to the grave and back with Christ, what can stand in our way?

PAUSE TO REFLECT

C. Consider how Jesus and Israel were tempted to turn away from God in the desert. As you leave your teenage years and high school life, what temptations do you think you will face? It might help to recall the temptations you faced at other "desert times" in your life.

D. As the Israelites traveled through the desert, God's presence was visible to them in the form of a pillar of cloud during the day and a pillar of fire at night. How has God been present in your life, especially during times of change and challenge? If you have not noticed God's presence, think of a time of change or challenge and imagine how it might have been different if you had been aware of God's presence with you.

↳ YOUR RESPONSE

TUNING IN TO GOD'S PRESENCE

Most of us find that talking about trusting God is easier than actually practicing it—and that's especially true during times of change and uncertainty.

Sometimes experiencing God's constant presence helps us to trust in it. Just as we have to tune in to radio waves before we're aware of their presence all around us, we usually have to "tune" ourselves to be aware of God's presence in our daily lives.

The following journal exercise can help you do just that. Try it every day for a few weeks.

- Start by writing down the two or three most significant things about your day. Whatever comes to mind first is probably the most significant. It might be something great or small, good or bad.

- For each significant thing, ask, "Why does this stand out from the rest of the day?" Reflect on the deeper meaning of each significant thing, recording your answer in writing.

- For each significant thing, ask, "How was God involved?" and record your answer in writing. Often your first answer might be, "God wasn't involved." But the Christian tradition affirms that God is indeed present in the people, things, and events of our lives. If God's presence isn't immediately obvious, say a simple prayer: "God, how were you present in this event?" Open yourself to God's response in silent reflection.

- Read what you have written about your day's experiences and reflect on them. Then allow yourself to respond to God in prayer. This prayer may take any form, such as praise, thanksgiving, petition, or awareness of the need for repentance (paraphrased from Gerald T. Chinchar, "Journal Keeping in the Inquiry Period," in *Catechumenate*).

PAUSE TO REFLECT

E. Answer this question in light of the reflection you've done during this chapter: "How would I like to respond to change?"

WHERE DO I GO FROM HERE

Who Do I Want to Be?

Discovering Your True Identity

The summer of my seventh-grade year, my family and I took a vacation to our "home" in Nigeria, where my parents were born. My cousin and I were playing cards, talking girl talk, and relating our most embarrassing moments. . . . I told her the story of how I was laughed at because of my weird name. I thought it was pretty funny, but she didn't laugh. She had the most serious look on her face, then she asked me, "Immaculeta Uzoma Achilike, do you know what your name means?" I shook my head at her and that's when she started laughing. I thought she was making fun of me, and as I started to leave she said: "Immaculeta means 'purity,' Uzoma means 'the good road' and . . ." Having heard her words, I stopped walking away and turned around in amazement. "What does Achilike mean?" I asked. After a long pause she calmly said, "Achilike means 'to rule without force.'" I was astonished and pleased. I never knew what my name meant.

My name is Immaculeta Uzoma Achilike. I am the daughter of first-generation Nigerian immigrants. I am the daughter of hardworking and brave parents. My name means "to rule without force." My grandfather was a wealthy man of generous character. When I say my name in Nigeria, people know me as the granddaughter of a wealthy man of generous character. They know me by my name. There my name is not embossed on any pencil or vanity plate. It is etched in the minds of the people.

My name is Immaculeta Uzoma Achilike. (Imma Achilike, "Why Couldn't I Have Been Named Ashley?")

As a child, Immaculeta ("Imma") Uzoma Achilike let her identity—who she was in her own eyes and the eyes of others—be defined more by other kids than by herself. Constantly teased about her unusual name, she wished for a more "normal" name, like Ashley. But as she discovered her family roots and the meaning of her name, she began to see herself in a new light.

Imma's struggle with her identity is common. At one time or another, most people wish they were someone else, or they let other people define their identity, or they put on a "false front," denying their true identity so others accept them. And like Imma, almost everyone has moments of profound self-discovery—in fact, fully realizing our true identity is a lifelong process.

As you prepare for life after high school, you are probably more concerned about what you will do with your life than who you will be. What you want to do with your life is an important concern, one that we will consider in chapter 6. But it's all too easy to get overly focused on doing: "Now I need to get into a good college. . . . Now I need to find romance. . . . Now I need to find a job . . . a house . . . a retirement plan. . . ." As worthwhile as all these things are, what we are doing doesn't mean much if we lose track of who we are becoming along the way. Young adulthood is an especially important time to reflect on who we want to be because all the changes and challenges of this time—leaving old roles, relationships, and routines to try on new ones—help to shape our adult identity.

Michael Gurian tells a story that illustrates the importance of reflecting on who we are becoming. As an American Jew, he grew up hating Germans for what they did to his relatives during the Holocaust. During a life-changing visit to the former Nazi death camp at Dachau, in Germany, he realized his hatred had led him to become someone he didn't want to be:

> I was so grief-stricken in that camp that I could not weep until hours later. I left after a day of experience, but returned the next day. I felt fear and revulsion but pushed onward toward something I could not define until after hours and days of standing at the racks of torture, walking the yards, and listening to the whispers. I was surprised, in the end, to feel not hatred for the German people, but something amazing—forgiveness. . . .

I was a young man in search of a soul, and I found my own. . . . I remember standing in the Dachau yard, taking an inventory of my identity. "Who are you?" I asked myself. "If you stop hating and fearing the Germans, who are you?" I wrote in my journal for hours, and indeed for days after that. (*A Fine Young Man*, pp. 165–166)

Imma and Michael searched their deepest selves with courage and honesty, and in doing so, they discovered something more about their true identity, in all its dignity. The questions they posed have the power to reveal your true identity, too: What is the real meaning of your "name," your true identity? Who are you? If you are stripped bare of your fears, of others' definitions, of the false fronts you present to others, who are you?

PAUSE TO REFLECT

A. If your name were listed in the dictionary, what definition or definitions would you like to have follow it?

B. Conduct a survey of five or more people who know you pretty well. Ask each person to write a definition of who you are. (You will get the most honest responses if you give each person time and space to write a thoughtful definition of you.) How do their definitions compare to your own? What part of their definitions do you accept—and what do you reject?

WHERE DO I GO FROM HERE

If we were to sum up the Bible's understanding of identity, we might say that we are what is in our heart:

> The heart is the dwelling-place where I am, where I live; according to the Semitic or Biblical expression, the heart is the place "to which I withdraw." The heart is our hidden center, beyond the grasp of our reason and of others; only the Spirit of God can fathom the human heart and know it fully. The heart is the place of decision, deeper than our psychic drives. It is the place of truth, where we choose life or death. It is the place of encounter, because as image of God we live in relation: it is the place of covenant. (*Catechism*, no. 2563)

Imma and Michael are good examples of this truth. Imma had taken other kids' teasing to heart, allowing it to partially shape her self-definition. Once she let go of others' definition of her, though, she found something more at the heart of her being. Likewise, the hatred and fear in Michael's heart had made him a slave to the Nazis; by passing through the desert of the Dachau death camp, he was able to let go of that old identity and find something more in his heart—something that, amazingly, enabled him to forgive his enemies.

This "something more" lies in the innermost heart of every person: it is the dignity that comes from being created in the image of God, and it is the foundation of our identity:

> Then God said, "Let us make humankind in our
> image, according to our likeness." . . .
>> So God created humankind in his image,
>>> in the image of God he created them;
>>> male and female he created them.
>
> (Genesis 1:26–27)

Nothing defines our identity more than the truth that we have been created in the image of God, and nothing can take that away from us.

CREATED IN THE IMAGE OF GOD

When we truly believe that we are created in the image of God, we can begin answering the question "Who am I?" in these ways:

- I am a creation of God's love.
- I am made to love.
- I am invited to heaven.
- I am free to respond to God's invitation.

I AM A CREATION OF GOD'S LOVE

We are not the product of chance, nor are we self-made; instead, as the passage from Genesis points out three times, God created us. We are a creation of God's love. Blessed Julian of Norwich, a fourteenth-century English mystic, had a beautiful vision of this truth:

> [The Lord] also showed me a little thing, the size of a hazelnut, lying in the palm of my hand. It seemed to me as round as a ball. I gazed at it and thought, "What can this be?" The answer came thus, "It is everything that is made." I marveled how this could be, for it was so small it seemed it might fall suddenly into nothingness. Then I heard the answer, "It lasts, and ever shall last, because God loves it. All things have their being in this way by the grace of God." (*Julian of Norwich: Showings*, p. 130)

God is an eternal exchange of love between the three persons of the Trinity—Father, Son, and Holy Spirit. That love is not self-contained but constantly overflows, bringing all of creation—including ourselves—into being. The most basic thing we can say about our identity is that we exist because God loves us, even if we fail to recognize that love.

I AM MADE TO LOVE

The creative force of God's love begins to shed light on what it means to be created in God's image. If God is love, and we are made in God's image, then we are made for love:

> God is love and in Himself He lives a mystery of personal loving communion. Creating the human race in His own image and continually keeping it in being, God inscribed in the humanity of man and woman the vocation, and thus the capacity and responsibility, of love and communion. Love is therefore the fundamental and innate vocation of every human being. (John Paul II, *Familiaris Consortio*, no. 11).

People often think of love as a warm feeling or "being nice" to others. That may be true sometimes, but Christian love is a decision, an act of the will, before it is a feeling. It is a choice to act for the good of the other—whether that choice makes us feel good or not. Jesus's sacrifice on the cross didn't feel good, nor was he being nice when he rebuked his followers or the public authorities. But those were acts of love because they were decisions to act for the ultimate good of others. God's love is the model for Christian love: it is always creative, life giving, and aimed at the good.

Just as a hammer is made for building and a knife is made for cutting, everything about us is made for loving. To be created in the image of God means that love is our most basic purpose for being, and we are happiest when we live out what we are made for.

I Am Invited to Heaven

God created us so he could love us and so we could freely return his love and share it with others: "God himself is an eternal exchange of love, Father, Son, and Holy Spirit, and he has destined us to share in that exchange" (*Catechism,* no. 221). God calls us to begin living in that exchange of love now, so one day we might share in it fully. This full, direct experience of the love shared between the persons of the Trinity and all the saints is what we call heaven.

When it's described in the abstract like this, God's call to heaven might seem uninspiring. Jesus offered a more appealing image when he compared heaven to a wedding banquet where everyone is an invited guest (see Matthew 22:1–14). Heaven is like a banquet featuring everything that is good and beautiful, everything that makes us laugh with delight. All of that and infinitely more is folded into heaven's constant exchange of love—God, Creator of the universe, holds it all in his hand like Julian's hazelnut.

Nor does heaven reduce people to a boring uniformity; on the contrary, those who live in heaven "retain, or rather find, their true identity, their own name"[1] (*Catechism,* no. 1025). Fully charged with God's creative, life-giving love, we finally become most fully ourselves, and the false images that separate us from one another come crashing down once and for all.

Our invitation to heaven has profound implications for our identity: We are more than our bodies; rather, we are body and soul (*Catechism,* nos. 362–367). This means we cannot look at ourselves as two separate parts, body and soul. Instead, we are one body-soul. Our full identity is not destined for the grave; rather, we are created for eternal life in heaven.

These claims about our fundamental identity will radically alter our lives if we truly believe them. Instead of living for ourselves, we are suddenly able to live for others; instead of working toward a long retirement, we find ourselves working toward heaven; instead of hating our enemies, we find ourselves strangely free to love them. "I was a young man in search of a soul, and I found my own," Michael Gurian said at the beginning of this chapter. God's grace at work in his soul allowed him to forgive his enemies, freeing him to rise above the circumstances life handed him.

I Am Free to Respond to God's Invitation

In Jesus's parable about the wedding banquet, not everyone accepts the invitation to the party—these people believe they have better things to do, such as taking care of business concerns. Like the invited guests in the parable, we are also free to accept or reject God's invitation to heaven. Knowing that love is our "fundamental and innate vocation" doesn't mean we are forced to love; by definition, love is not love unless it is freely chosen. That's why freedom is an essential part of our identity as people created in the image of God—if we weren't free, we wouldn't be able to love. Just as no one can take away our creation in the image of God, so no one can take away the freedom to shape our own heart. Even when we feel trapped by our circumstances, we are always free to choose how we will respond to those circumstances.

Choosing Our Heart

What would you be like if you reflected God's image in a way that most fully expresses all that is good in you? That identity seems foreign to most of us. Who feels personally loved by the Creator of the universe on most Monday mornings? Who feels like they're made for love, especially after a long day?

If we read further in the Book of Genesis, we learn that sin shattered the image of God in humanity—the free choice to turn away from God, the source of our being. Our identity may not be obscured by pain, fear, and hatred, like Michael Gurian's was, but it is obscured by sin nonetheless. That's why our identity in the image of God can seem so foreign, as if the person we're called to be is a stranger to us. The good news is that the image of God in humanity is restored in Jesus Christ—and it can be restored in us if we live in him.

That's the choice that lies behind many of the choices of young adulthood (and all of life, really): will we choose what brings us closer to discovering our true heart? It's a question that we will continue to explore in various forms as we work through the rest of this book.

PAUSE TO REFLECT

C. Take some time to examine your heart. What do you find there that keeps you from fully realizing your true identity?

D. Look back at the self-definition you wrote in question A on page 24. Now write another self-definition that describes what you would be like if you reflected your identity as someone created in the image of God.

E. Imagine that you were to die five years from now. Write a newspaper obituary that reflects who you hope to have become in the next five years.

WHERE DO I GO FROM HERE

THE SACRAMENT OF HONESTY

As important as it is to reflect on our identity in light of who we are becoming, it's no easy task. Among the major obstacles on the journey toward realizing our true selves are sin and self-deception—fooling ourselves about who we really are. If we don't pause occasionally to examine our hearts, we risk waking up one day to find we don't like who we're becoming.

One amazing tool to help us be honest with ourselves and God is the sacrament of Penance and Reconciliation (also known as confession). It offers us the opportunity to examine our hearts and confront the sin and self-deception that prevent us from becoming the "something more" that God is calling us to be. "Penance is the sacrament of honesty," explains Edward Vacek, a Jesuit priest:

> To counteract our well-developed ability of self-deception, we . . . need confession. Indeed, we should want to confess because, in effect, through the sacrament, God says: "You name it; I'll forgive it." With this offer in mind, it is to our advantage to face up to our sinfulness. While self-deception keeps us crippled, honesty heals. Just as a desire not to think of ourselves as sinners fosters the skill of self-deception, so too a desire to know ourselves as forgivable sinners leads to self-discovery and then to liberation. We feel safe enough to bring our sins out in the open because we trust that God wants to heal, not humiliate us. ("Do 'Good People' Need Confession?" in *America*)

"Only the Spirit of God can fathom the human heart and know it fully," the *Catechism* says (no. 2563). In confession, God helps us know ourselves more fully—not to shame us, but to heal the sin in our hearts so we might be more open to his transforming love. Confession is not so much a self-report on all the bad things we've done as it is a way of asking our Creator's help in becoming more fully alive.

As you move through this book, you will want to consider receiving the sacrament of Penance and Reconciliation. You might want to prepare for it in this way:

Keep a notebook beside your bed. At the end of each day, spend a few minutes recalling the events of the day. As you do, jot down a few notes about what you did that reflects the type of person you want to be; also record those moments when your words or actions were not consistent with who you want to be.

When you are ready to receive the sacrament of Penance and Reconciliation, prepare yourself by reviewing your notes. What patterns do you notice? How do you most clearly reflect God's image? What sinful habits prevent you from becoming who God is calling you to be? The answers to these questions can be a starting point for your confession.

Many people don't go to confession because they find it intimidating. If you feel nervous, ask someone you trust to recommend a priest who works well with young adults; you might also ask what to expect. Let the priest know you haven't received Reconciliation in a while—he'll probably be glad to guide you through the sacrament in a friendly way.

After receiving the sacrament of Penance and Reconciliation, continue the practice of taking notes about your day. Do you notice any changes in yourself as a result of the "sacrament of honesty"?

PAUSE TO REFLECT

F. Answer this question in light of the reflection you've done during this chapter: "Who do I want to be?"

WHERE DO I GO FROM HERE

How Will I Find Happiness?

The Question

What Does It Mean to Be Happy?

WE ALL WANT TO LIVE HAPPILY.[1]

(Saint Augustine of Hippo,
Catechism, no. 1718)

Obviously, I want to be successful. Success to me means happiness, and happiness means having people appreciate you for who you are, not for your money or anything else. I don't necessarily have to be famous and make a huge impact all across the world, but I would like to be some inspiration for people to look on and be like, "Look, she's strong, she's doin' her thing. It's not impossible." My biggest hope is that I keep strong morals and a sense of what's important to me, that I can look back on my life and say, "I'm a good person," and that I'm as happy with myself in seventy years as I am right now. (Renee, age 17, in Audrey Shehyn, *Picture the Girl*, p. 66)

Everyone wants to be happy, and that desire motivates every act of every person, according to the seventeenth-century mathematician, theologian, and inventor Blaise Pascal. Stated another way, Pascal would argue that no one ever knowingly chooses something that will make him or her less happy; even self-destructive choices are made because they appear better than other options.

Does that claim seem true in light of the choices you have made so far today? Maybe you didn't want to get out of bed this morning—but you got up anyway because you calculated you'd be happier in the long run.

(Getting out of bed beats the hassle of missing the bus or being late to school or work, for instance.) Your decisions about what to wear, what to eat, and what to say to others were probably also based on what seemed most pleasing to you at the time, even if you didn't consciously think through your decision.

The quest for happiness guides our life decisions just as much as it does our day-to-day decisions. Consider, for instance, how Renee's understanding of happiness will guide the decisions she makes as she enters young adulthood. How about you? What does happiness mean to you, and how will you find it?

PAUSE TO REFLECT

A. Are you happy now? Why or why not?

B. Think about the happiest times of your life and briefly describe them in writing. What is it about these times that made you happy? Based on these experiences, what does happiness mean to you?

C. As you look forward to the rest of your life, what do you think will make you happy?

WHERE DO I GO FROM HERE

THE HUNGER FOR HAPPINESS

Before we can find happiness, we need to know what we're looking for. Look up *happiness* in the dictionary, and its definition probably will include a state of well-being, contentment, or satisfaction. In other words, happiness is the sense that everything is complete; we want nothing more. This can easily be misinterpreted to mean we are happiest when our immediate desires have been fulfilled.

It's no wonder so many people look to wealth, power, social status, health, and good looks as keys to happiness. After all, anyone who has those things is probably better able to fulfill his or her desires than someone without them. By this logic, star football players, fashion models, and business leaders should be among the happiest people on earth.

But that turns out not to be the case. The many scientists who study what makes people happy say these things "have precious little to do with the satisfaction we experience," according to a *Newsweek* magazine article summarizing happiness research:

> Health, wealth, good looks and status have astonishingly little effect on what the researchers call "subjective well-being." Even paraplegics and lottery winners typically return to their [previous levels of happiness] once they've had six months to adjust to their sudden change of fortune. People living in extreme poverty are, on average, less happy than those whose basic needs are met. But once we cross that threshold, greater wealth stops making life richer. People in Japan have nearly nine times the purchasing power of their neighbors in China, yet they score lower in surveys of life satisfaction. In America, . . . real income has doubled since 1960. We're twice as likely to own cars, air conditioners and clothes dryers, twice as likely to eat out on any given night. Yet our divorce rate has doubled, teen suicide has tripled and depression has increased tenfold. Somehow, we're not cut out for the ease that comes with wealth. (Geoffrey Cowley, "The Science of Happiness")

Our hunger for happiness is much like our hunger for food—it's satisfied for a while, but it always comes back. We tend to think, "If only _____, then I could be happy." Once we get what we want, we're happy for a while, but soon there's a new "blank space" in our lives we think we need to fill to be happy. Maybe that's why the authors of the U.S. Declaration of Independence referred to the "pursuit" of happiness—as if it were something we are always chasing after but not guaranteed to hold onto for long.

MADE FOR NOTHING LESS THAN EVERYTHING

So is the human search for happiness futile—or is it possible to find an enduring happiness, a happiness that will satisfy our hunger once and for all?

Jesus answers this question in a story in the Gospel of John (chapter 6). Seeing that the crowds are hungry, Jesus feeds thousands of people by miraculously multiplying a few fish and loaves of bread. The next day, the crowds come after Jesus looking for more bread. But Jesus tells them that they are looking for the wrong sort of food: "Do not work for the food that perishes, but for the food that endures for eternal life," he says (verse 27).

"Sir, give us this bread always," the people reply (verse 34).

"I am the bread of life," Jesus says. "Whoever comes to me will never be hungry, and whoever believes in me will never be thirsty" (verse 35). The people respond to this teaching with doubt, but they are even more skeptical about what he says next: "Those who eat my flesh and drink my blood abide in me, and I in them. Just as the living Father sent me, and I live because of the Father, so whoever eats me will live because of me" (verses 56–57).

The crowds came to Jesus looking for something to feed their hunger. They would have been happy to settle for ordinary bread, but Jesus knew that neither bread nor anything else that the earth has to offer can satisfy the deep hunger of the human heart. That's because God placed an empty space inside each person—an emptiness that opens onto the infinite and the eternal. That emptiness is too large to be filled by anything less than God, who holds all the beauty and goodness of creation in the palm of his outstretched hand. "The desire for God is written in the human heart," the *Catechism* says, because the human person is created by God and for God. "Only in God will [the human person] find the truth and happiness [he or she] never stops searching for" (no. 27).

The human person is made to "want it all," to not be satisfied by anything less than everything. That is what Jesus offers the crowd when he offers himself to them: "Why settle for ordinary bread?" he seems to say. "Why not have food that satisfies your hunger forever? Why not have it all?" And that is what we get when Jesus abides in us. The image of eating Jesus's flesh and blood startled his listeners, but it emphasizes the totality and intimacy of his relationship with us. If we are open to receiving him, he gives himself to us completely: body and blood, soul and divinity; he holds nothing back. When the eternal Son of God lives in us, our hearts open wider to beauty, goodness, and happiness that endure forever.

LIVING IN JESUS'S LOVE

The Gospel of John records that many of Jesus's disciples responded to his invitation by leaving him: "This teaching is difficult; who can accept it?" they said (6:60). Even if the happiness that Jesus offers sounds appealing, the disciples' reaction might give us pause—what is it, exactly, that makes Jesus's invitation so difficult to accept?

The image of "eating" Jesus suggests a radical acceptance that makes him the center of our being; we are not only to eat his body and blood, but to believe in his word (see John 6:35). To make Jesus the heart of our identity in this way is to give ourselves as completely to him—heart and mind, body and soul—as he gives himself to us.

Giving our whole selves to Christ is something few people have the courage to do, but we make a beginning when we receive, with an open heart, the sacraments of initiation: Baptism, Confirmation, and the Eucharist. All these sacraments initiate us into life in Christ, but the Eucharistic celebration holds a special place among them. The Church calls the Eucharist the "source and summit of the Christian life"[2] (*Catechism*, no. 1324). It is in the Eucharistic liturgy that we hear Jesus's words and affirm our belief in them. And it is in the Eucharist that we enter into communion with Christ by giving ourselves to him as completely as he gives himself to us.

At first, this might sound like a piece of cake, especially if receiving the sacraments involves nothing more than just showing up at church at the right time and going through the motions. But although abiding in Jesus Christ begins with the sacraments, it doesn't end with them. Jesus wants our whole lives, not just the few hours we spend in church.

The Gospel of John's account of the Last Supper helps to clarify what abiding in Jesus means. When the synoptic Gospels (Matthew, Mark, and Luke) recount the story of the Last Supper, they focus on the institution of the Eucharist: Jesus shares bread and wine with the Apostles, saying they are his body and blood offered up for the salvation of the world. In John's account of the Last Supper, however, the action focuses on Jesus washing his Apostles' feet.

Travelers' feet got pretty dirty in those days—after all, the roads weren't paved, and few people wore closed shoes. Washing the feet of a guest was a traditional act of hospitality, but it was usually a servant who did this dirty work. So when Jesus "got up from the table, took off his outer robe, and tied a towel around himself" (John 13:4) to wash his Apostles' feet, they were understandably startled—Peter even refused, at first, to have Jesus wash his feet.

"Do you know what I have done to you?" Jesus asked them when he finished. "You call me Teacher and Lord—and you are right, for that is what I am. So if I, your Lord and Teacher, have washed your feet, you also ought to wash one another's feet. For I have set you an example, that you also should do as I have done to you" (John 13:12–15).

Abiding in Jesus begins with our worship of him, especially in the Eucharist. But Jesus got up from the Eucharistic table to serve his Apostles; fully living in Jesus means we leave the Eucharistic table to do as he did. At its heart, abiding in Jesus Christ means living in love. Later in the Gospel, Jesus tells his Apostles:

> "As the Father has loved me, so I have loved you; abide in my love. If you keep my commandments, you will abide in my love, just as I have kept my Father's commandments and abide in his love. I have said these things to you *so that my joy may be in you, and that your joy may be complete.*

> "This is my commandment, that you love one another as I have loved you. No one has greater love than this, to lay down one's life for one's friends." (John 15:9–13, emphasis added)

STANDING AT HEAVEN'S GATE

Jesus invites us to live in his love so our "joy may be complete." But winning that enduring joy requires some hard work and sacrifice on our part. To be clear, living in Jesus does not mean turning our back on everything we enjoy about life, like friendships, satisfying work, good food, alone time, the thrill of an intense ball game, or even shopping for ourselves. Jesus undoubtedly enjoyed many of these things himself.

But living in Jesus's love does mean asking whether we are settling for these things when we could have more. Especially during times of transition, it can be easy to try filling the emptiness inside ourselves with "ordinary bread," or worse, instead of the bread of life; the Israelites certainly substituted other things for God many times during their journey through the desert. The ordinariness of our daily bread may be comforting, but Jesus calls us to set it aside whenever we find ourselves substituting it for the bread of life.

Is such sacrifice worth it? The experience of the saints, as well as more ordinary people, confirms the truth of Jesus's promise. Consider the story of Olivia Zehner, a high school student from East Syracuse, New York. During a class trip to Washington, D.C., she chose to give up her ordinary bread (quite literally) to feed the hunger of her heart:

> On the last day, a Sunday morning, I was on my way to get something to eat, and I came across a young . . . homeless man. He approached me and the group I was with, and he began to entertain us with his unique ability to rap. Most of my friends kept going, but my friend Brad and I decided to stay and listen to the man. His talent amazed me. When he was through, we applauded, and he asked us for money. I thought about this for a second and then asked him if a hot lunch would interest him more. I took the last bit of my spending money and bought the man a hot dog with everything on it, a bag of chips, and a soda. The man was so grateful, and as he walked away, he said, "Thank you, and God bless you."
>
> And God did bless me. My heart was so overwhelmed with happiness and love. . . . I realized then that for me, helping others in need was how the love of God was revealed in my heart. I realized it was something I could do and be happy with for the rest of my life. This experience did not tell me exactly what I want to do "when I grow up," but it did show me the road I eventually will travel. ("Finding My Road," in *Every Step of the Way*, p. 123)

Loving a stranger is hard; loving an enemy, as Jesus calls us to do (see Matthew 5:44) is even harder. That's why living in Jesus begins with the sacraments; we need his help to really live in his love.

Over time, the hard work of love becomes easier as it opens our hearts ever wider. Those who practice living in Jesus's love long enough sometimes find that their eyes are even opened to the beauty of heaven in the world around them. Heaven is not so much a place as it is the experience of being perfectly united in love with each other and the Holy Trinity; it is "the ultimate end and fulfillment of the deepest human longings, the state of supreme, definitive happiness" (*Catechism,* no. 1024). Thomas Merton, the famous monk and spiritual writer, had such a vision one day while stopped at a traffic light at the intersection of Fourth and Walnut streets in downtown Louisville, Kentucky:

> I was suddenly overwhelmed with the realization that I loved all those people, that they were mine and I theirs, that we could not be alien to one another even though we were total strangers. It was like waking from a dream of separateness. . . . There is no way of telling people that they are all walking around shining like the sun . . .
>
> It was as if I suddenly saw the secret beauty of their hearts, the depths of their hearts, where neither sin, nor desire, nor self-knowledge, can reach the core of their reality, the person that each one is in God's eyes. If only we could all see each other that way all the time! . . . The gate of heaven is everywhere. (*Conjectures of a Guilty Bystander,* pp. 140, 141, and 142)

Sin may prevent us from fully entering heaven in this life, but whenever we accept Jesus's invitation to live in his love, we have already begun to taste the happiness of heaven.

PAUSE TO REFLECT

D. Jesus told a parable in which he compared the Kingdom of heaven to a great feast; not all the invited guests show up, though, because they have other things to do. Read the version of this parable told in the Gospel of Luke 14:16–24, then reflect on this question: What might be your equivalent of "oxen," "land," or "marriage"?

E. Reread Olivia's story on page 42, then reflect on times when you have had a similar experience of happiness as a result of loving someone. Jot down as many examples as you can remember. What does your reflection reveal to you about where you find happiness in life?

WHERE DO I GO FROM HERE

↳ Your Response

Fasting: Making Space for God

Our discussion of food, hunger, and happiness provides a good introduction to the practice of fasting. To fast is to give up something we normally view as essential; doing so exposes the emptiness inside us so it might be filled with the presence of God. In that way, the ultimate goal of fasting isn't self-denial, but a deeper happiness—even though we might feel hungry along the way. Your experience of fasting will be most fruitful if you keep this ultimate purpose in mind.

Start your fast by setting aside something that "takes up space" in your life, something that feels essential but really isn't—that is, something that means a lot to you but is not necessary for your health or well-being, something other than your relationship with God and others. Some possibilities are listening to music, watching television, shopping, eating out, surfing the Internet, and just staying busy—all of which you can give up by setting aside some time every day to be quiet and still.

During your fast, you will probably experience an emptiness that you may be tempted to fill with whatever you gave up. Whenever you encounter that emptiness and temptation, turn it into a space for holding fast to God by asking him to fill you. You may want to pray these lines spoken by Jesus during his fast in the desert, substituting whatever you are giving up for the word *bread:*

> "'One does not live by bread alone,
> but by every word that comes from the mouth of God.'"
>
> (Matthew 4:4)

Pause to Reflect

F. Answer this question in light of the reflection you've done during this chapter: "What does happiness mean to me, and how will I find it?"

WHERE DO I GO FROM HERE

How Will I Find Love and Friendship?

→ The Question

We All Need Somebody

There is a type of a sixth sense that exists only between the closest of friends. The best lessons cannot be read from a textbook; we must experience the joys and trials of this journey with our friends and look inside of their souls to see life's truths. Great friends are extensions of ourselves and guide us through this obstacle course called life. (Amber Brown)

Great friends are defined by the song, "Lean on Me." The song describes someone who is understanding and willing to make sacrifices, someone who wants to help his friend get through a tough time. This is what a perfect friend is. Such genuine care, once given, tends to become mutual, for "we all need somebody to lean on." However, no one is always going through a tough time, which brings up the second part of a great friend. A great friend should also be capable of keeping good times rolling. (Anonymous)

Every person I meet and will be meeting is important to me because they'll affect my life in some way. But I see a friend as someone I trust and value. A great friend is that and more. A great friend knows everything about you.

You can tell a great friend from a regular friend. It's like finding your soul mate . . . your souls are so closely connected that you are practically bonded as one. You just know and that's the greatest part. To me, a great friend is someone who has walked with me through the darkest times of my life and is still standing with me. (Michelle Aposto)

"We all need somebody." That's certainly true at a basic survival level. Unlike animals who can safely abandon their young at birth, humans are social animals who need one another to survive. That's one of the reasons people have lived in communities since prehistoric times.

But "we all need somebody" at a deeper level than mere survival. We all need friends—people whose commitment to us is based on more than what they can get from us. The high school students quoted on the previous page name some of the reasons for this deeper need. And Michelle's comment about "soul mates" reflects an uncommon quality of friendship—the sense that our horizons are expanded, making us more as persons than we would be alone.

Young adulthood doesn't diminish our need for friends—in fact, you might find yourself needing somebody to lean on more than ever as you encounter the changes coming up in your life. Friendship also is vital as we begin to explore relationships that someday may lead to marriage. Any romantic relationship must first be founded in a true and deep friendship.

Good friends can be companions for your journey through the desert between adolescence and young adulthood. Take a moment to consider: How will you find love and friendship in the next five years?

PAUSE TO REFLECT

A. What does it mean to be a friend?

B. By the definition you gave in question A, who are your friends now and why? Do you count your family members as friends?

C. How do you expect to find love and friendship in the next five years?

⤷ The Covenant

At the beginning of this book, we said the transition from adolescence to young adulthood was like the Israelites' journey through the desert on their way to the Promised Land. Over the past few chapters, we've reviewed the course that Christian faith charts through that desert. So far our map through the desert contains three main reference points:

- The desert of change isn't necessarily something to be feared if we trust God to be our guide (chapter 1).
- God's love is our source, our destination, and the heart of our identity (chapter 2).
- We can find real, lasting happiness by living in Jesus's love (chapter 3).

Clearly, love plays a major role in the course that God has charted for us through the desert. Until now, we've talked about love in pretty abstract terms. As we turn to the question of friendship, though, our understanding of Christian love begins to take on flesh and blood. In many ways, the call to love can be understood most fully within the context of friendship. If we can understand the qualities of true friendship, we'll have a better understanding of Christian love—and that will bring us closer to realizing our true identity and finding enduring happiness.

The Call to Love and Friendship

Jesus made love the center of his teaching, and he often connected love to friendship. In the Gospel of John, the connection is explicit:

> "This is my commandment, that you love one another as I have loved you. No one has greater love than this, to lay down one's life for one's friends. You are my friends if you do what I command you. I do not call you servants any longer, because the servant does not know what the master is doing; but I have called you friends, because I have made known to you everything that I have heard from my Father." (15:12–15)

And in the Gospel of Luke, a lawyer asks Jesus to name the greatest commandment of the covenant. "You shall love the Lord your God with all your heart, and with all your soul, and with all your strength, and with all your mind; and your neighbor as yourself," Jesus answers (10:27).

When the lawyer presses Jesus to define what he means by "neighbor," Jesus responds with the parable of the good Samaritan to illustrate what it means to be a neighbor, or friend (see 10:30–37). The parable is ironic because the Jews scorned the Samaritans as religious inferiors who didn't worship God in the proper way. And yet it is the Samaritan, not the two Jewish religious men, who acts rightly by stopping to help the man left half-dead at the side of the road. In the parable of the good Samaritan, Jesus teaches that our worship of God is meaningless if we don't love one another. Christian friendship focuses not so much on what we can get, but on what we can give.

The desert of major life transitions can be a lonely place; in that loneliness, it can be easy to let the question "Who will love me?" dominate our lives. But Jesus reminds us that there is no shortage of people who need our friendship. The solution to our loneliness is to be like the good Samaritan, reaching out to those on the side of the road whom everyone else passes by. Jesus doesn't call us to ask, "Who will love me?" Instead, he calls us to ask, "Who can I love? Who needs my love?" Those who focus on loving others soon find that love returned one hundredfold.

THE BUILDING BLOCKS OF FRIENDSHIP

Let's take a step back to one of the questions you considered above: What does it mean to be a friend? Drawing on Jesus's teaching, as well as the comments of the young people quoted previously, we can begin to name five basic building blocks of friendship: commonality, love, commitment, intimacy, and mutuality.

COMMONALITY

Most friendships begin when we discover that we have something in common with someone else—common interests, circumstances, or personality traits, for instance. Practically speaking, it's difficult to form a friendship with someone with whom we have little in common.

The Christian call to love does not necessarily call us to form lasting friendships with everyone we meet—that's not physically possible, at least during our life on earth. (Heaven is another matter.) But Christian love does call us to treat all people we meet as neighbors—that is, as if they were our friends—even if we don't expect to develop a lasting, mutual friendship with them. That's because everyone shares a common origin in God (see *Catechism,* no. 360); all people are made in the image of God and continue to be loved by God regardless of their circumstances or actions. That's why Jesus calls us to love one another as much as he has loved us, treating even strangers with the same compassion the good Samaritan showed.

LOVE

At the heart of friendship is love—not necessarily romantic love, but the type of love that wants what is good for the other and actively works to bring that good about for the other. The word love has many different meanings, not all of which correspond to the type of love to which God calls us, so it might be helpful to name some basic characteristics of Christian love.

Love brings out the best in the other. True friends bring out the best in each other. When we see friends through the eyes of love, we see past their flaws and masks to find the shining goodness deep inside them; we point out that goodness to them and help our friends bring that goodness to the surface where others can see it, too.

Love sacrifices for the other. True love requires sacrifice—that is, giving to the other without expecting something in return. Giving so that we might receive something in return is bartering, not love. "No one has greater love than this, to lay down one's life for one's friends," Jesus says (John 15:13). Most of us are called to make sacrifices on a smaller scale: the good Samaritan sacrificed his time and money for the sake of the stranger; a married couple sacrifices other possibilities for their lives to live out the possibilities of their commitment to each other; someone else might cancel their plans to stay by a friend in trouble.

Love seeks the good. As we discussed in chapter 2, people sometimes mistakenly believe that love is all about being nice. Love involves acceptance and respect, but always within the limits of what is good for the other. It does not imply being "nice" or silent in the face of something that might harm the friend. Nor does it imply that we ought to take abuse from another; doing so is as bad for the abuser as for the abused.

COMMITMENT

Love is often thought of as a warm feeling toward another person; by this standard, love and friendship last as long as they make us feel good.

It's easy to be a friend to someone who makes us feel good, and a lot of relationships are mostly based on the social status, good looks, wealth, or fun personality of one or both of the persons involved. When those things change, the relationship dies.

But Christian love is a decision, an act of the will, before it is a feeling. It is a choice to act for the good of the other—whether that choice makes us feel good or not. True friendship, by extension, involves a commitment to the good of the other person regardless of that person's circumstances.

The level of commitment we have toward a friend depends on the seriousness of the relationship. Married couples have a different level of commitment toward each other than do casual friends, for example. But the story of the good Samaritan illustrates that we are called to be committed to the good of every person we meet, whether we like that person or not. Many people consider Dorothy Day to have been a modern saint because of her commitment to care for the people left "half-dead by the side of the road" in the United States. And yet, her love for those people didn't come automatically. Sometimes, she said, she felt that

> the burden gets too heavy; there are too many of them; my love is too small; I even feel with terror, "I have no love in my heart; I have nothing to give them." And yet I have to pretend I have.

> But strange and wonderful, the make-believe becomes true. If you will to love someone, you soon do. You will to love this cranky old man, and someday you do. It depends on how hard you try. *(On Pilgrimage)*

INTIMACY

"I have called you friends, because I have made known to you everything that I have heard from my Father," Jesus tells his disciples (John 15:15). Likewise, Michelle says in her comments at the beginning of this chapter that "a great friend knows everything about you." Both Jesus and Michelle are talking about intimate friendships. In our modern culture, the word *intimacy* often implies sexual activity. Actually, the root of *intimacy* is the Latin word *intimus*, meaning "inmost" or "deepest." Intimate relationships are those in which people reveal their innermost being, the deepest reality of who they are, to one another. This type of friendship is rare because it requires a high degree of trust. Intimate friendships are also valuable because they allow others to help us more fully discover our true identity. We're lucky if we have a few intimate relationships during our lives on earth. Only in heaven, where our true identity is fully revealed, will we experience total intimacy with God and one another.

In this life, it's impossible for us to be *totally* intimate with everyone we meet. But we are called to practice a basic level of intimacy even with strangers. This type of intimacy is Christian hospitality, and it is able to welcome the stranger as a friend because it recognizes that the image of God is present within every person. This does not mean sharing intimate details of your life with everyone you encounter. Rather, we are called to be open and inviting to everyone we encounter. Jesus says that whenever we welcome the stranger, we also welcome him (see Matthew 25:35–40).

MUTUALITY

True friendship is always a two-way street; it blossoms only when our care for the other is returned. In a friendship marked by mutuality, both people:

- share roughly the same type and level of love and care for each other
- share about the same level of intimacy
- have a say in decision making
- are about equally committed to the relationship

No relationship is reciprocal in perfectly equal proportions. But when mutuality is missing, relationships are lopsided. A relationship isn't a true friendship if one person always calls all the shots, or if one person shares her deepest self but the other does not, or if one person feels intense love but the other feels only affection.

That's why Jesus tells his disciples, "You are my friends if you do what I command you" by loving one another (John 15:14). Jesus is not saying that his love for us is conditional; he continues to love us even if we turn away from him. But it is only when we return Christ's love that our relationship with him rises to the level of friendship.

As Christians, we are called to treat all people as if they were friends— that is, with the Christian love and respect they deserve as human beings created in God's image. But Christianity doesn't require us to enter a friendship with everyone who wants to be friends with us, nor is it realistic to expect that everyone we like will become a true friend.

"Dare . . . to Be a Real Friend"

The building blocks of commonality, love, commitment, intimacy, and mutuality can serve as a good foundation for any relationship, whether between near strangers, casual friends, or marriage partners. As you move into young adulthood, the building blocks can strengthen the friendships you have and help you develop new ones.

While these building blocks are a strong foundation for friendship, no friendship is as strong or enduring as one that is grounded in both persons' friendship with God. Fr. Henri Nouwen, an internationally known author and lecturer, eloquently explains why this is so:

> Many of your friendships grew from your need for affection, affirmation, and emotional support. But now you must seek friends to whom you can relate from your center, from all the places where you know that you are deeply loved. Friendship becomes more and more possible when you accept yourself as deeply loved. Then you can be with others in a non-possessive way. Real friends find their inner correspondence where both know the love of God. *There spirit speaks to spirit and heart to heart.*
>
> True friendships are lasting because true love is eternal. A friendship in which heart speaks to heart is a gift from God, and no gift that comes from God is temporary or occasional. All that comes from God participates in God's eternal life. Love between people, when given by God, is stronger than death. . . .
>
> Dare to love and to be a real friend. The love you give and receive is a reality that will lead you closer and closer to God as well as those whom God has given you to love. (*The Inner Voice of Love,* pp. 80 and 81)

Pause to Reflect

D. Which of the five building blocks of friendship will be most important in helping you strengthen your current friendships over the next five years? Why?

E. What qualities or characteristics will you look for as you seek new friends as a young adult?

F. What would a romantic relationship look like if it were based on the five building blocks of friendship?

OFFERING THANKS FOR FRIENDS

"A friendship in which heart speaks to heart is a gift from God," Henri Nouwen says. Whenever we receive a gift, the best response we can offer is one of thanks. Set aside some time to offer thanks for an important friendship, whether with a peer, a parent, or another relative. Reflect on these questions and record your responses in writing:

- What do you share in common with your friend?
- How do you and your friend love each other? That is, how do you bring out the best in each other?
- How have you sacrificed for each other? Can you think of times when you or your friend has worked for the good of the other—even if it meant not being nice?
- How have you demonstrated your commitment to each other?
- In what ways have you revealed your innermost selves to each other? What has that meant for your friendship?

When you are finished, use your writing as the basis for a prayer of thanksgiving to God for your friendship. Consider sharing your reflections with your friend as a thank-you gift.

PAUSE TO REFLECT

G. Answer this question in light of the reflection you've done during this chapter: "How will I find love and friendship?"

WHAT WILL I TAKE WITH ME?

PACKING FOR THE JOURNEY

What would you do if someone left you at a bus station with only $35, a one-way ticket and three changes of clothes, and asked you to rely on God's grace for the next month? Last April, I took such a leap of faith as part of my Jesuit training.

I remember my fears as the bus left St. Paul. Where would I sleep? What would I eat? Who would become part of this journey of faith? Would I return safely? . . . Like Ignatius of Loyola, I was venturing into the unknown, relying only on divine providence. . . .

The first days on the road were unsettling but led me to turn to God in new ways. I got into the habit of praying the rosary each morning. After a few days, I gave up worrying where the next meal or bed would come from. God met all these needs and brought me much joy in the process. When I ran out of money on Vancouver Island, a kind woman invited me to dine with her family and then paid my boat fare. In Seattle, a homeless woman offered to share her lunch with me and showed me a list of food shelters. I stayed in Seattle for three weeks working with homeless Native Americans. I saw God work through them in simple and profound ways. They taught me about living humbly, loving deeply and being faithful to my true self. They brought me to powwows and invited me into their lives. . . . The Risen Christ had shown me his face in the poor and marginalized, and invited me to a deeper relationship with him. (John Meehan)

John is one of the many Jesuit novices that the Society of Jesus has sent on a month-long pilgrimage with only a few clothes, a bus ticket, and $35. That pilgrimage recalls Jesus's instructions to his followers to "take nothing for your journey, no staff, nor bag, nor bread, nor money—not even an extra tunic" (Luke 9:3). Packing so light might seem risky to the average traveler, but it's a good way for the novices to deepen their trust in God's loving care. By the end of their journey, they know that the only travel essentials they need are ones they can't pack in a bag. John Meehan named some of them, like faith and prayer; others might include hope, courage, and the support of others. With resources like these, a person can go anywhere.

Sometime in the next few years, you will probably find yourself packing your bags full of all the things you want to take along as you leave home. You don't need to worry right now about what to take or how to cram it all into the back of your car. But now isn't too soon to begin packing the real essentials of your life's journey—the ones that won't fit into a suitcase. So take a moment to think about the journey ahead . . . what will you need to take with you?

PAUSE TO REFLECT

A. Imagine that you are embarking on a month-long trip with only $35 and a change of clothes. What personal qualities would you consider essential for your journey?

↳ THE COVENANT

We could list dozens of travel essentials for the Christian journey, but here we'll focus on just three: the virtues, prayer, and community. Jesuit novice John Meehan relied on all three of these essentials during his pilgrimage, and they can help you on your journey, too.

THE VIRTUES

"I remember my fears as the bus left St. Paul," John says. "Where would I sleep? What would I eat? Who would become part of this journey of faith? Would I return safely?" To overcome those fears, John drew on his virtues—habitual ways of thinking and acting that promote good relationships with ourselves, God, and others. As you read the following descriptions of some basic virtues, see if you can imagine how each might have helped John on his pilgrimage—and how they might help you on your journey.

- **FAITH** prompts us to believe wholeheartedly in God and to align our will with God's will. A living faith leads us to love both God and one another.

- **HOPE** enables us to rely on God's help in times of difficulty and loneliness, rather than relying on our strength alone. Hope is rooted in the radical belief that God is constant and undefeatable, as demonstrated in Christ's Resurrection. With hope, we're less likely to make decisions based only on what will lead to our immediate happiness; instead, hope enables us to make decisions that lead to true, lasting happiness.

- **LOVE** is the virtue by which we respond to God's love by giving ourselves to God with all our heart, soul, strength, and mind (see Luke 10:27), and by which we give ourselves to others because of our love for God. Thomas Aquinas called love the mother of all other virtues. The Apostle Paul said it "binds everything together in perfect harmony"(Colossians 3:14).

- **PRUDENCE**, or **WISE JUDGMENT**, reins in and controls all the human virtues (see *Catechism*, no. 1806). Prudence can be thought of as the "look before you leap" virtue, helping us to look ahead to the consequences of our choices before we make them. Prudence draws on the gift of reason and practical experience to figure out the best course of action.

- **TEMPERANCE** is the virtue of self-control. People without temperance unthinkingly indulge in violence, risky behavior, alcohol, sex, material consumption, overeating, and so on—even when such things clearly aren't good for themselves or others. Temperance enables us to control these impulses and emotions instead of being controlled by them.

- **JUSTICE** is usually called "righteousness" in the Bible; it refers to acting rightly toward God and neighbor by giving them what they are due. Our duty toward God, of course, is to offer praise and worship in our words and everyday actions. Our duty toward other people is to treat them with the respect they deserve as beings created in the image of God. In this context, respecting other people means more than just being polite. It also means making sure all people have what they need to fully become all that God intended them to be.

- **FORTITUDE** basically means "strength"; it is the strength we need to overcome fear, even the fear of death, so that we are free to do what is good. This is the virtue that helped John Meehan overcome the fears and doubts he had about his pilgrimage. Fortitude might also be described as the courage to do the right thing.

Noelle Frigo had a dramatic experience of God's grace working through the virtues during her senior year of high school. After learning she was pregnant, she decided to have an abortion. Her boyfriend and another friend accompanied her when she went for the procedure:

> We had decided to drive 150 miles to get the abortion. We didn't want to risk anyone finding out about it at home. I felt pretty firm in my choice. I wasn't feeling any indecision. It was very quiet in the car and I had fallen asleep. We must have been driving for an hour or more when I woke with a start. The first thing that met my eyes were the words, "Listen to Jesus, he knows," spray-painted on an overpass. "Stop the car," I said. I just knew God was prompting me to reverse my decision. The spray-painted words reminded me that Jesus would help me with the pregnancy and any choices that went along with it. From that moment on, I never regretted changing my mind.

Faith made it possible for Noelle to respond to the spray-painted message on the overpass; hope enabled her to believe that God would always help her with the challenges she faced; love enabled her to choose the good, even at great personal sacrifice. And fortitude gave her the strength and courage not only to follow through with her decision, but to follow Christ in all aspects of her life.

How do we pack these essentials for the journey? It's impossible to acquire the virtues overnight. To some extent, the virtues are like any other skill—they require practice before they come easily to us. The people around us, our community, also help us develop the virtues; we're more likely to practice the virtues our friends, family, and neighbors commonly practice. Ultimately, though, the virtues are gifts of God's grace, and one of the most basic ways to nurture them is to ask for them in prayer.

PRAYER

Prayer played an important role in the success of John Meehan's pilgrimage: "I got into the habit of praying the rosary each morning," he says. "After a few days, I gave up worrying where the next meal or bed would come from. God met all these needs and brought me much joy in the process." Prayer is essential to Christian faith because it is the basis of a personal relationship with God (see *Catechism,* no. 2558), who is the source of our being and our guide for the journey of life.

Describing prayer as the basis for our personal relationship with God has some important implications for how we go about the practice of prayer. "You are my friends," Jesus said (John 15:14); if we take that seriously, then we will invest at least as much time, energy, and attention in that friendship as we do in our human relationships. It also suggests that our prayer relationship with God ought to reflect some of the basic elements of friendship:

- Our creation in the image of God is the common basis that makes it possible for us to relate to God, even though God is our Creator.
- Love animates our friendship with God; God's love for us prompts us to love him and one another in return.
- God remains perfectly committed to us, even when we fail in our commitment to God: "Man may forget his Creator or hide far from

his face; he may run after idols or accuse the deity of having abandoned him; yet the living and true God tirelessly calls each person to that mysterious encounter known as prayer" (*Catechism,* no. 2567).

- Our relationship with God becomes intimate through prayer, because in prayer God reveals himself to us and reveals the heart of our identity to ourselves.

- Our relationship with God must be mutual: Just as God gives himself wholly to us in the person of Jesus Christ, we are called to give our whole selves to God; and just as God listens to us, we need to be silent long enough to hear God's word to us.

- In one important way, our relationship with God is not like an ordinary human friendship: God is our Creator, Lord of the universe, and we are not. "Fear of the Lord" is a biblical phrase that describes the healthy awe and respect we owe God. Approaching prayer in a spirit of humility opens us up to receive the gift of prayer from the Holy Spirit: "*Humility* is the foundation of prayer," the *Catechism* notes. "Only when we humbly acknowledge that 'we do not know how to pray as we ought,' are we able to receive freely the gift of prayer"[1] (no. 2559).

There are many, many different forms of prayer; just as a strong friendship has many dimensions, so too our relationship with God is strongest when we explore that relationship in many ways. First and foremost, we are called to pray as part of the community of faith because the liturgy of the Church is "the outstanding means whereby the faithful may express in their lives, and manifest to others, the mystery of Christ and the real nature of the true Church" (Pope Paul II, *Sacrosanctum Concilium,* no. 2). The Liturgy of the Hours and the rosary are two other ways of joining the whole Church in prayer. Privately, we can meditate on God's presence before the exposed Eucharist or an icon; we can "pray twice"[2] by singing (*Catechism,* no. 1156); we can listen to God's word in the Scriptures or other holy writing; we can keep a written journal of our prayers; we can pray traditional prayers, especially the Lord's Prayer; we can dance in praise of God (see 2 Samuel 6:14) or create art that praises God; or we can simply contemplate God in silence.

Most significant, if prayer is a personal relationship with God, and God is always present to us, then we pray whenever we acknowledge that presence (see *Catechism,* no. 2565). Everything we do—even the mundane work of everyday life—has the potential to be a prayer if we do it for God.

COMMUNITY

At first it might seem strange to name community as an essential for the journey; after all, John Meehan made his Jesuit pilgrimage alone. But look at his story again and you'll notice how he repeatedly reached out in friendship to others: the family on Vancouver Island, the homeless woman in Seattle, the Native Americans. The word *community* contains the words *common* and *unity;* as the *Catechism* says, "Because of its common origin [in God] *the human race forms a unity"* (no. 360). With the eyes of Christian faith, John was able to recognize this common connection with complete strangers. He wouldn't have had a successful pilgrimage without the help of this community of strangers and newfound friends.

But John also relied on another community during his journey—the Church, which is the community of those who live in Christ, both on earth and in heaven. Their common life in Christ forms a bond between members of the Church that transcends time, space, and even death. As long as John had access to these different communities, he was never truly alone on his pilgrimage.

Many people live by the slogan "I'm spiritual but not religious." In other words, they believe in God but do not belong to a community of believers. People do receive support for their spiritual growth through friends with a similar viewpoint. But it's difficult to grow into a mature faith without a Christian base. Life in the Church community is essential to Christian faith because, as people made in the image of the Holy Trinity, we are made for communion with God and one another; God's call to covenant is also a call to community (see *Catechism,* nos. 759–766).

It shouldn't be surprising that God chose to achieve his plan of salvation through community. God established his covenant with the Israelites as a whole people, not as individuals (see *Catechism,* no. 781). Jesus, too, handed his saving mission on to a community of followers, the Church.

The Church is no ordinary community; what makes it unique is Jesus's promise that he will continue to be present in the gathering of his followers: "Where two or three are gathered in my name, I am there among them" (Matthew 18:20). People sought Jesus's healing power in his person when he walked the earth; today, people can find that same healing presence in the Church when his followers remember and celebrate the Paschal mystery in the sacraments.

The Church is kind of like a big family that we're born into through the waters of Baptism. But just because we're born into this family doesn't mean we'll necessarily feel comfortable in it. The basic elements of friendship listed in chapter 4 can help us feel more at home in the Church; three of those elements are especially important:

- **Commonality.** Finding our home in the Church requires nurturing a mature faith because a common faith in Jesus Christ is what binds the Church together.

- **Mutuality.** Mutuality reminds us that our relationship with the Church has to be one that balances what we receive with what we give. We should move beyond the question "What can the Church do for me?" to ask "What can I do for the Church?"

- **Commitment.** If we believe that Christ is really present in the gathering of his followers, then our commitment to Christ requires an equally strong commitment to the Church. While such a strong commitment is essential, it isn't always easy to maintain.

For one thing, we might find the Church challenging our own beliefs and practices. That's not necessarily a bad thing, though. Just as it's impossible to excel at a sport without challenging our physical limits, it's impossible to grow in faith without challenging our spiritual limits. Instead of immediately rejecting such challenges, we should respond to them as we would respond to the challenges friends and family members pose—by listening, asking questions, seeking to understand, and sharing our own thoughts. Growing in faith is a lifelong process, one made easier by the virtue of humility.

Our commitment to the Church might also be challenged by the fact that, although Christ's presence makes the Church holy, it is also made up of human beings. It's not a community for perfect people, but for sinful people who want to become more holy. Anyone who is committed to life in the Church is likely to encounter that sinfulness sooner or later. But Christ is present in the Church even when the sinfulness of its members makes seeing his presence difficult. Remember how Jesus's Apostles abandoned him just as he needed them the most? Even though they fled him, Jesus never abandoned them. In fact, the resurrected Christ sent the Holy Spirit to dwell among them and continue Jesus's ministry.

The same is true today: Christ remains committed to the Church in spite of the sinfulness of its members, because only through Christ's presence in the Church can such sinfulness be transformed. Like Christ, our presence in the Church has the potential to transform sinful situations when we respond to them with love, courage, and respect.

The virtue of humility reminds us that none of us is perfect, which is why the Church is an essential for the journey. We need Christ, and we need each other, to help us in our weaknesses, to pick us up when we fall, and to carry us when we lack the strength to go on. Together, we can make it through any desert to find the Promised Land on the other side.

PAUSE TO REFLECT

B. Take an inventory of the virtues presented in this chapter. Which are strongest in you? Which do you need to work on in preparation for young adulthood?

C. Virtues are habitual ways of thinking and acting that promote good relationships with ourselves, God, and others. With that definition in mind, what other virtues do you possess that were not addressed in this chapter?

D. How does the quality of your friendship with God compare to your other friendships? How do you see prayer fitting into your life as a young adult?

E. What gifts or talents do you possess that the community of Jesus's followers, the Church, needs?

↳ YOUR RESPONSE

A PRAYER OF THE HEART

Prayer is essential to Christian life, and yet the difficulty of prayer prevents many Christians from developing as deep a friendship with God as they would like. If you have a hard time praying, here's a simple yet powerful prayer you can recite anywhere: "Lord Jesus Christ, Son of God, have mercy on me, a sinner." An even shorter version is: "Lord Jesus Christ, have mercy on me."

This is known as the Jesus Prayer, or the prayer of the heart. The method of the prayer is simply to recite it constantly throughout the day—verbally at first, and then in the silence of the heart. Reciting the Jesus Prayer accomplishes several things:

- By invoking the name of Jesus, it makes Jesus's power present to us; it is by the power of the name of Jesus that his followers are able to cast out devils (see Luke 10:17) and to heal the lame (see Acts 3:6–7).

- It grounds our prayer in humility by admitting our sinfulness and our need for Jesus. It is rooted in the cry of the blind beggar Bartimaeus: "Jesus, Son of David, have mercy on me!" (Mark 10:48); like Bartimaeus, people who recite the Jesus Prayer find themselves healed and transformed, able to see the world and the people around them in a whole new light (see *Catechism*, no. 2616).

- By constantly reminding us of Christ's presence throughout the day, it enables us to pray by offering the events of the day to him.

The Jesus Prayer may seem like rote recitation at first, but practiced long enough, it becomes habitual. Ultimately, the words of the prayer become transparent, so that our attention shifts from reciting words to experiencing the presence of Jesus more and more fully in everything we do.

PAUSE TO REFLECT

F. Answer this question in light of the reflection you've done during this chapter: "What essentials do I need to take into my young adulthood?"

6

WHAT PATH WILL I CHOOSE?

↳ THE QUESTION

FINDING YOUR PATH

> Finding my true vocation won't happen until I have found myself. When I was little, I loved singing and I wanted to be an opera singer. Then with the age of obsession with pink came ballet. However, my lack of talent in dance and my interest in so many other things made me change my mind in kindergarten from ballerina to teacher. Then in sixth grade, I discovered how hard it was to discipline disrespectful kids. So, I thought and I wondered. What did I love doing that would in some way help others and be good for the world? Then came the idea of being a doctor. As a doctor I could have a stable job, be well rounded, and most of all help people. Plus, I began to fantasize, I could work in third world countries from time to time. . . . As I move on I keep developing and changing my mind. I will stay open to God and He will be my North Star. (Clémence Sullivan)

Throughout this book, we have said the transition to young adulthood is like the Israelites' journey through the desert to the Promised Land. We have said that while the desert may sometimes be lonely and frightening, it can also be a place where we encounter God, who reveals our true identity and guides us toward our Promised Land, a life filled with love, friendship, and enduring happiness. And we have named a few essentials to take along on the journey.

Now that we are better prepared to set out, we return to the question we first raised in chapter 2: What will you do with your adult life? Clémence has the right idea when she talks about making God her guiding star; in the past few chapters, we've explored the general direction in which God calls us. But while that might help us narrow our choices, it still leaves a lot of possible paths to choose from. All the options Clémence named—becoming a dancer, teacher, or doctor—are potentially good ways of spending one's life. But she also recognized that those options might not be the best way to spend her life.

Given all the possibilities for your life, how will you decide which paths to take? Start by taking a moment to dream about those possibilities and where they might lead you.

PAUSE TO REFLECT

A. Imagine yourself as an adult twenty-five years from today. An eighteen-year-old, perhaps your child or the child of a friend, asks you to talk about your life and how it came to be what it is. Write a response, using some or all of the following questions to guide you:

- What does your environment look like—your home, your work, your leisure?
- Who are the most significant people in your life?
- What have you accomplished?
- What have you contributed to the world, and what do you still hope to contribute?
- What image of you do your friends have?

DISCERNING YOUR VOCATION

Most people make major life decisions based on some form of logical analysis. James VanOosting, dean of the college of arts and sciences at Seton Hall University, in South Orange, New Jersey, identifies two common strategies: comparing advantages and disadvantages, and doing the odds (James VanOosting, "Vocation Education," in *America*).

Advantages versus disadvantages. One approach involves comparing the advantages of a certain choice to the disadvantages. If someone is deciding whether to become a lawyer, for example, the person might write a heading labeled "advantages." Under it, the person might list personal satisfaction, a high income, and a favorable social standing. Under "disadvantages" the person might list stress and the time and expense of law school. A person says yes to a particular choice only if the advantages of the choice seem to outweigh the disadvantages.

Doing the odds. Another approach involves weighing the odds that a particular choice will be successful. Using this approach, someone might ask, "What are the odds I will make it into law school, pass the bar exam, and advance in my career?" The choice being considered is pursued only if the odds of success seem good.

Logical analysis is a valuable, God-given tool for making decisions, so you might find aspects of these approaches helpful in making decisions about your life. But VanOosting points out that for those who live in the light of Christian faith, decisions can't be reduced to a simple logical analysis because such an approach ignores God's role as the source, sustainer, and final destination of each person's life. People who make decisions in the light of faith take into consideration God's plan for their lives, the destiny that God calls them to fulfill.

God's call to each person is his or her vocation, a word that comes from the Latin *vocare,* meaning "to call." We've already outlined the basic elements of that call in previous chapters: God calls every person to find enduring happiness through communion with him (see *Catechism*, no. 27). Because we enter into that communion through love, the first and most fundamental vocation of every human being is to love (2392).

God calls each of us to fulfill this basic vocation in a way that is unique to the individual character and circumstances he has given us. No one else in the world possesses the gifts, talents, and opportunities you do. Your vocation is to use these unique gifts to bring about the particular good no one else can accomplish in every area of your life—your work, relationships, roles, and so on.

In contrast to a purely logical approach, Christian decision making begins by asking, "What is the good that God is calling me to accomplish with my unique gifts and interests?" Christian decision making not only takes into account the advantages and disadvantages of each option, but it also trusts that God always wants to lead us to our greatest happiness. Christian decision making not only takes into account the odds of success, but it also trusts that all things are possible with God at our side.

This process of making decisions by looking for the good to which God calls us is known as discernment. Discernment is not about finding some detailed blueprint for our lives that God has hidden away from us. Nor are we limited to only one chance to "get it right." God wants us to fulfill our talents and potential (see Matthew 25:14–30) and offers us many ways of doing so, as well as room for growth. Catherine Bertrand, a School Sister of Notre Dame, assures us that "God is a God of multiple choices. There is no one way that is the only way" ("On Responding to God's Call," in *Origins*). As long as we are living our vocation to love as best we can, we are responding to God's call.

LISTENING FOR GOD'S CALL

Talk about listening for God's call might conjure up images of God calling Moses from the burning bush, or the angel Gabriel visiting Mary. Most of us won't hear God's call quite so directly, but that doesn't mean God isn't speaking to us. If you listen carefully, you will discover that God calls to you in many different ways.

THROUGH PRAYER

Prayer is an essential part of Christian discernment because it opens us to hear God's call more clearly—not only while we are praying, but in every aspect of our lives.

When we pray for God's help in discerning our particular vocation, we don't need to be shy about bringing our deepest desires to God in prayer. In fact, Jesus encourages us to do so: "Ask, and it will be given you; search, and you will find; knock, and the door will be opened for you" (Matthew 7:7). Jesus promises that, like a good parent, our Father will "give good things to those who ask him" (Matthew 7:11).

If we really trust that God wants what is good for us, then in addition to bringing our deepest desires to him, we will also listen to his deepest desires for us. We begin to do this by giving serious consideration to all the good possibilities for our life—even those that we might initially reject out of fear or selfishness. Instead of allowing those emotions to dictate our response to God's call, we can imitate Moses. When God called him to lead the Israelites to freedom, Moses balked, made excuses, and even questioned God—all of which were legitimate ways of praying (see *Catechism,* no. 2575). Even complaining to God is better than turning away from him if our complaint opens us to his transforming presence.

THROUGH YOUR HEART

One of the ways God speaks to us is through our heart, "our hidden center" that "only the Spirit of God can fathom" (*Catechism,* no. 2563). We begin to listen to God's voice in our heart by prayerfully considering our own deepest dreams and desires: Who do you want to be? What do you want to do with your life? What do you think would make you happiest?

Teacher, counselor, and spiritual director Thomas Hart notes that Christians often assume "what they want and what God wants are opposed, as if God were against them rather than for them." But if faith in God guides our lives, then this is not necessarily true: "If God loves us, then surely God wants us to be ourselves, to do what expresses our true selves, to have what is good and brings us genuine satisfaction" (*Spiritual Quest,* p. 138). It makes sense that our own desires might very well reflect God's desire for us.

Jamie Johnson, a college student, discerned her vocation in part by listening to her heart:

> Throughout my life I have been exposed to the arts in various ways—dancing in recitals, going to plays, viewing fine painting. As I participated in these activities my passion and love of the arts

grew, particularly for ballet. To me it is as if my truest self is revealed when I am dancing on stage. I feel art is not something that you keep to yourself, but something that you share with others. Although I am not certain exactly how my passion for the arts will manifest itself as a way to serve and witness in the world, I am going to continue on my path, expanding my knowledge of this area so that I might share it with others.

Discovering her true self was a strong indication to Jamie of where her vocation might lie. Mother Teresa's experience of discernment points to a similar test. As a young woman, she wondered whether God was really calling her to the religious life. She asked her confessor (a kind of spiritual mentor): "How can I know if God is calling me and for what he is calling me?"

"You will know by your happiness," her confessor replied. "If you are happy with the idea that God calls you to serve him and your neighbor, this will be the proof of your vocation. Profound joy of heart is like a magnet that indicates the path of life. One has to follow it, even though one enters into a way full of difficulties" (Mother Teresa, *My Life Serving the Poor,* p. 2).

As important as it is to listen to our hearts, we also need to be cautious about whether we are really hearing God's call. We can better hear God's voice in our hearts if we watch out for the following:

- Our vocation is rarely revealed in an instantaneous flash of insight. We may need to live with a particular possibility for days, weeks, or months before our hearts respond with profound joy to it.

- Others may have more influence over us than we realize. We need to avoid pursuing a choice to please friends or family members or because we're afraid of being ridiculed or looked down on. We may need to be discerning in the amount of influence we allow others to have over our choices.

- As we discussed in our exploration of happiness, the desires of our heart don't always lead to our ultimate good. Attachments to people, money, or social status can derail us from realizing our true vocation.

THROUGH THE NEEDS OF THE WORLD

Because our most basic vocation is to follow Christ's command to love God and neighbor, discerning our particular vocation means that in addition to considering our own dreams and desires, we need to ask, "What does the world need, and what gifts do I have that can fill that need?"

One of the ways we can hear how God is calling us to serve the world's needs is through the social teaching of the Church. That teaching identifies some of the basic requirements of justice: protecting the life and dignity of every human person; ensuring the right and responsibility of every person to fully participate in family and community life; safeguarding the basic human rights that are essential for a happy life; caring for creation; avoiding war and violence whenever possible; and so on.

Besides these fundamental requirements of social justice, we can also recognize the more ordinary, everyday things that the world needs: someone to make the toothpaste, balance the books, and sweep the streets. The world also needs people to bring it joy, beauty, and laughter.

In other words, attending to the needs of the world as we discern our vocation doesn't necessarily imply that God calls everyone to serve the world in the way Mother Teresa did, as she herself repeatedly acknowledged. She had this to say to the cast of a musical performance in Calcutta, India:

> Your work and our work complete each other. What we are doing is needed in the world as never before. You are giving them joy by your action and we are doing the same by service. And it is the same action whether you are singing and dancing and we are rubbing and scrubbing. You are filling the world with the love God has given you. (*The Joy in Loving*, p. 145).

In the Catholic tradition, any work that contributes to the good of the world is holy, no matter how insignificant it may seem. Even typing on a computer or operating heavy machinery can be a form of prayer, explains Robert Ellsberg: "According to the monastic perspective, each task has its own good. When we work with proper attention and respect for that good, our work assumes a prayerful quality, and we can say that God is present in it" (*The Saints' Guide to Happiness*, p. 43).

Contemporary American writer and theologian Frederick Buechner offers the following advice for discerning how these needs might correspond to our vocation:

> By and large a good rule for finding [the voice of God] is this: the kind of work God usually calls you to is the kind of work (a) that you need to do and (b) that the world most needs to have done. If you really get a kick out of your work, you've presumably met requirement (a), but if your work is writing TV deodorant commercials, the chances are you've missed requirement (b). On the other hand, if your work is being a doctor in a leper colony, you have probably met requirement (b), but if most of the time you're bored and depressed by it, the chances are you have not only bypassed (a) but aren't helping your patients much either. . . . The place God calls you to is the place where your deep gladness and the world's deep hunger meet. (*Wishful Thinking*, p. 95).

Besides the needs of the world, as Catholics we are also called to consider how our vocation serves the needs of the Church. Perhaps the most obvious ways of serving the Church are through a vocation to ordained ministry (the deaconate or priesthood) or religious life as a brother or sister. But marriage is also a vocation that serves the Church, as is the lay vocation that all Christians are called to by virtue of their baptism.

THROUGH OTHER PEOPLE

Finally, we can also hear God's call through the voices of other people, especially those who know and love us the most. Although no one can make our decisions for us, it is almost always helpful to check our own instincts against the perceptions of others. Friends, family, spiritual guides, and mentors such as a coach or teacher can sometimes point out gifts and talents you might not have fully realized you possessed. At other times, these people might save you from self-deception that would otherwise lead you down a dead-end road. Their support can provide you with the resources you need to persist in your true vocation when the going gets tough; conversely, their insight can help you realize when it's best to stop pounding on a closed door.

As you listen for God's voice in others, it's important not to allow the opinions of others to become a substitute for your own discernment process. In the end, God calls *you* by name, and you are the only one who can offer a genuine response.

PAUSE TO REFLECT

B. Look through the Bible for an example of someone whom God called. Briefly summarize who the person was, how the person was called, how she or he responded, and what the outcome of the response was. How might the person have answered differently by using one of the logical analysis approaches outlined in the chapter? What does this example say to you as you discern your own call?

c. Interview two adults who have made a vocational choice. Ask how they discerned their vocation. What advice do they have to offer for your own discernment?

YOUR RESPONSE

BEGINNING TO DISCERN

Discerning a vocation takes more than an hour or two; it usually takes several years to realize how God calls us to make a significant life decision, even if we are not always consciously discerning during that time. And in fact, the process of discernment never really ends because God is always calling us to something new.

With that in mind, take some time—ideally, a few days—to begin the practice of discernment by listening for God's voice in each of the following areas:

- Begin with prayer. Find a quiet place and spend some time praying to God. (Remember all the different types of prayer we listed in the last chapter.) You may want to use the words of people who responded to God's call in the Bible as a model for your prayer.

- Examine your heart for obstacles to discernment. What do you fear you might discover through your discernment? What do you think you couldn't give up? What expectations do you or others have about what you will do with your life? How do your circumstances (for example, limited finances or a disability) seem to limit your options?

- Question the desires and dreams of your heart. What were your childhood dreams, and why did you give them up? What are your dreams now? What are your unique gifts and talents? How do your dreams and gifts fit into your vocation to love?

- Consider the world as you know it. What do you think the world needs more than anything? What do you think the Church needs most? What most stirs your interest and compassion? Where do your own joy and the world's needs meet?

- Think of everyone who knows you well. What do these people say about you? If you asked them to list your strengths and shortcomings, what would they say? Who can serve as a model for the type of person you want to become? How might these people support and challenge you as you discern your vocation?

You may want to jot down your responses to each question, or you might prefer simply to sort through these questions mentally. What patterns or themes seem to emerge as you begin discerning your vocation?

PAUSE TO REFLECT

D. Answer this question in light of the reflection you've done during this chapter: "How will I decide what path to choose?"

LIVING THE QUESTIONS

WHERE DO I GO FROM HERE

WHICH WAY TO THE REST OF MY LIFE?

↳ TAKING CHARGE OF YOUR DIRECTION IN LIFE

We started this book with Alice's simple question about which way she should go. In the chapters that followed, you spent some time living with that question in different forms. Now it is time to return to that original question and begin developing a map through the desert in the form of a covenant statement.

WHAT IS A COVENANT STATEMENT?

A covenant statement is a lot like a personal mission statement. Individuals and organizations typically create mission statements to describe who they are (their identity), what they want to accomplish (their goals), and the means by which they intend to accomplish those goals (their direction). Once it is written, a mission statement reminds them to stay true to their identity and to stay headed in the direction of their goals.

In other words, mission statements help people take charge of their identity and direction rather than just leaving these things to chance or the influence of other people.

Like a mission statement, a covenant statement describes our identity, goals, and direction, but it does so in light of the Covenant to which God called Israel:

> You have seen what I did to the Egyptians, and how I bore you on eagles' wings and brought you to myself. Now therefore, if you obey my voice and keep my covenant, you shall be my treasured possession out of all the peoples. Indeed, the whole earth is mine, but you shall be for me a priestly kingdom and a holy nation. (Exodus 19:4–6)

Jesus repeated this call to Covenant in a new way:

> "As the Father has loved me, so I have loved you; abide in my love. If you keep my commandments, you will abide in my love, just as I have kept my Father's commandments and abide in his love. I have said these things to you so that my joy may be in you, and that your joy may be complete.

> "This is my commandment, that you love one another as I have loved you. No one has greater love than this, to lay down one's life for one's friends. You are my friends if you do what I command you." (John 15:9–14)

These words are spoken to each of us; they are spoken to you now (see *Catechism*, no. 357). God stands before you speaking these words much like a lover proposing marriage. But just as friendship and marriage cannot exist without mutuality, so too does the call to covenant require our response, a response of faith and love. "Everything that the Lord has spoken we will do," was the Israelites' simple response to God's call to Covenant (Exodus 19:8). When we offer that "yes" of faith and love to God's proposal, we enter into a covenantal relationship with him.

The purpose of creating a covenant statement is twofold:

- The process of creating the statement helps us consciously take charge of our response to God's call. We may have a vague sense of responding to God by "being good," but developing a covenant statement forces us to think about what that means for our lives more specifically.

- Once it has been developed, a covenant statement serves to remind us of the commitment we have made to God, ourselves, and others, so we can carry it out in our lives. In this sense it becomes a sort of map, guiding us to the other side of the desert.

No covenant statement or mission statement can be the final word on your life, of course. As you travel along, you will want to refine it in light of newfound wisdom or changed circumstances. Rather than thinking of it as the final word, think of your covenant statement as helping you take the first steps in the right direction on a long journey.

CREATING YOUR COVENANT STATEMENT

Now it's time to actually develop your covenant statement. There is no one right way to approach this process—it's your statement, after all.

Even so, you will probably find the following guidelines useful for creating a really valuable covenant statement, one strong enough to help you through the next few years.

Preparing to Create Your Covenant Statement

Before you begin to actually create your covenant statement, you may want to do the following:

- Give yourself enough time to do this well. You might come up with a decent first draft in an hour (especially if you have really spent time with the questions in this book), but more likely, you will need to try out several versions before you settle on a covenant statement that really captures what you want to say. You might even want to set it aside for a few days to think it over before committing yourself to a final version.

- Review your responses to the questions in this book. Use a highlighter to mark passages or phrases you want to incorporate into your covenant statement. Notice any patterns or trends in your responses—do certain ideas keep coming up? Did your responses change over time?

- Quickly review this book, highlighting ideas or quotes you want to incorporate into your covenant statement.

- Gather any additional materials you think might be useful for creating your covenant statement—the Bible or the *Catechism,* a novel or song that has especially influenced you, words of wisdom from a friend or relative, and so on.

- Consider using a high-quality paper, special pens or computer fonts, or symbols or pictures that are important to you. You may even prefer to record your statement on videotape, audiotape, or a CD-ROM—although if you do, you will want to put down your statement in writing as well.

As you write your covenant statement, do so in a spirit of prayerful discernment: tune your ear to be open to hearing God's voice through prayer, your heart, the needs of the world, and the voices of other people who know you well.

A FRAMEWORK FOR YOUR COVENANT STATEMENT

The shorter your covenant statement is, the more meaningful and useful it is likely to be; it should be just long enough to say what is necessary. Keeping it short will force you to choose what is most important and will make it easier to remember and practice. You may need to write a long covenant statement at first just to get all your thoughts out; once that is done, though, use the process of discernment to identify what is really most important and set the rest aside. For most people, a useful covenant statement isn't more than a page long. If it's short enough to memorize, even better.

Remember that a covenant statement describes your identity, your goals, and your means for accomplishing those goals, all in light of God's call to covenant. The following brief review of what it means to live in the covenant provides a broad framework for developing your covenant statement:

IDENTITY. A covenant statement recognizes that God gives us our fundamental identity. In the part of your covenant statement that describes your identity, think about who God has made you to be. Who are you, at your best? How are you an image of God? What unique characteristics, gifts, and talents has God given you? As you work on this part of your covenant statement, it may help to review your responses to the questions in chapter 2. If you have not already done so, you may also want to ask people who know you well to describe your basic identity.

GOALS. A covenant statement recognizes that heaven is our ultimate destination and that we are called to begin living in heaven now. Remember from chapter 2 that heaven is the place where we find happiness by living in the exchange of love between God and all those who are united with him, and it is the place where we become most fully our true selves. As you work on this part of your covenant statement, think about how your goals bring you closer to heaven. Who is God calling you to be? What good things are you uniquely able to accomplish? You will probably want to focus especially on your responses to the questions in chapters 3, 4, and 6 as you develop this part of your covenant statement.

MEANS. A covenant statement recognizes that God is our guide through the desert, the means by which we reach the Promised Land;

just as God provided the Israelites with everything they needed on their journey, he will provide us with everything we need on our journey, too, if we ask. Think of this part of your covenant statement as providing a basic map for getting from where you are now to your goals. How will you stay connected to God through prayer? Who will travel with you as mentors on your journey? What God-given virtues will you need? You may find it helpful to draw on your responses to the questions in chapters 1 and 5 as you develop this part of your covenant statement.

TIPS FOR WRITING YOUR COVENANT STATEMENT

It is time to write your covenant statement. Start by unpacking all the elements you have been tucking away for your journey. To get started, lay out each of the following items:

- your "Pause to Reflect" answers from each chapter
- any additional reflections you did that you might find useful
- comments that are significant to you from mentors in your life

Draw on those materials as you compose your covenant statement, as you respond to God's call in writing, describing who you understand yourself to be and who you hope to become in relation to God, others, and self, and taking into account your own unique identity, values, gifts, and dreams.

Develop a first draft of your covenant statement using your responses to the reflection questions at the ends of sections. Here are some practical suggestions to guide your work:

- Keeping your statement short will force you to choose what is most important and will make remembering and practicing your covenant easier. If you have more to say than will fit in a concise covenant statement, you may want to write a separate, detailed explanation of the statement. Just because a statement is short in its final form does not mean that it cannot be long in its rough drafts.

- Like anything worth doing, developing a good covenant statement takes time. If you feel stuck or not quite satisfied with what you have written, set it aside to think about it for a while. Don't be afraid to revise it or even to try several different versions.

The visual presentation of your covenant statement should reflect the time and effort you have invested in it. Consider selecting a high-quality paper, using special pens or computer fonts, or incorporating symbols or pictures that are important to you.

Beyond that framework, the final look and feel of your covenant statement is up to you.

A PRAYER FOR THE JOURNEY

God is the great Questioner, as the pages of the Bible attest: "Where are you?" (Genesis 3:9); "Is anything too wonderful for the Lord?" (Genesis 18:14); "What troubles you?" (Genesis 21:17); "Whom shall I send?" (Isaiah 6:8). If you listen closely, you might hear God's voice in the questions you have about your life, too. However the question is worded, it is always an invitation to a more intimate relationship with him and to the deep happiness that can be found only in his presence.

As you worked on your covenant statement, perhaps you came across a few questions for which you had no satisfactory answer. It is true that answers are important; our lives unfold from our answers to such questions, after all. But not having an answer for every question—or getting them wrong, as Israel did so often—is not necessarily a cause for despair; more important is our "yes" to God's invitation, and our willingness to turn to him for help as we live the questions. Our covenant response isn't the end of our journey, but rather a first step in the right direction.

Here is a prayer by Thomas Merton that elegantly expresses this truth. Perhaps you can make it your own as you prepare for your journey into young adulthood:

My Lord God,

I have no idea where I am going,

I do not see the road ahead of me.

I cannot know for certain where it will end.

Nor do I really know myself,

and the fact that I think that I am following your will

does not mean I am actually doing so.

But, I believe that the desire to please you

does in fact please you,

and I hope that I have that desire in all I am doing.

I hope I will never do anything apart from that desire.

And I know that if I do this,

You will lead me by the right road,

though I may know nothing about it.

Therefore, I will trust you always,

though I may seem lost in the shadow of death.

I will not fear,

for you are ever with me,

and you will never leave me

to face my perils alone.

(THOUGHTS IN SOLITUDE, P. 83)

ACKNOWLEDGMENTS

The following students contributed written pieces for this book: Clémence Sullivan, John Meehan, Noelle Frigo, and Jamie Johnson.

The scriptural quotations contained herein are from the New Revised Standard Version of the Bible, Catholic Edition. Copyright © 1993 and 1989 by the Division of Christian Education of the National Council of the Churches of Christ in the United States of America. All rights reserved.

The material labeled *Catechism of the Catholic Church* or *Catechism* in this book is quoted or adapted from the English translation of the *Catechism of the Catholic Church* for use in the United States of America, numbers 357, 2563, 221, 1025, 362–367, 2563, 1718, 1324, 1024, 360, 1806, 2558, 2567, 2559, 1156, 2565, 360, 759–766, 781, 2616, 27, 2392, 2575, 2563, and 357, respectively. Copyright © 1994 by the United States Catholic Conference, Inc.—Libreria Editrice Vaticana. Used with permission.

The excerpt on page 7 is from *Alice's Adventures in Wonderland and Through the Looking-Glass,* by Lewis Carroll (New York: Bantam Books, 1981–1988), page 46. Copyright © 1981–1988 by Bantam Books.

The excerpt on page 10 is from *Letters to a Young Poet,* revised edition, by Rainer Maria Rilke, translated by M. D. Herter Norton (New York: W. W. Norton and Company, 1954), page 35. Copyright © 1954 by W. W. Norton and Company.

The excerpt by Jason Longo on page 11 is from "Reflections in the Yard" in *Our Boys Speak: Adolescent Boys Write About Their Inner Lives,* by John Nikkah (New York: St. Martin's Griffin, 2000), page 116. Copyright © 2000 by John Nikkah.

The excerpt by C. C. on page 11 is from *Turn Into the Wind: Prayers and Reflections by College Students,* edited by Shirley Kelter (Winona, MN: Saint Mary's Press, 1999), page 80. Copyright © 1999 by Saint Mary's Press. All rights reserved.

The "Three Stages of Change" on pages 14–15 is paraphrased from *Transitions: Making Sense of Life's Changes,* by William Bridges (Reading, MA: Addison-Wesley Publishing Company, 1980). Copyright © 1980 by Addison-Wesley Publishing Company.

The bulleted material on page 20 is paraphrased from "Journal Keeping in the Inquiry Period," by Gerald T. Chinchar in *Catechumenate,* volume 14, September 1992, page 18.

The story "Why Couldn't I Have Been Named Ashley?" by Immaculeta Uzoma Achilike, on page 22 is a 2004 "My Turn" winning essay, Newsweek Education Program, at *www.newsweekeducation.com,* accessed April 19, 2005. Copyright © 2004 by Newsweek, Inc. Used with permission.

The excerpt on pages 23–24 is from *A Fine Young Man: What Parents, Mentors, and Educators Can Do to Shape Adolescent Boys into Exceptional Men,* by Michael Gurian (New York: Penguin Putnam, 1999), pages 165–166. Copyright © 1998 by Michael Gurian.

The excerpt on page 27 is from *Julian of Norwich: Showings,* translated by Edmund Colledge and James Walsh (New York: Paulist Press, 1978), page 130. Copyright © 1978 by The Missionary Society of St. Paul the Apostle in the State of New York.

The excerpt from John Paul II on page 27 is from the "Apostolic Exhortation *Familiaris Consortio* of Pope John Paul II to the Episcopate to the Clergy and to the Faithful of the Whole Catholic Church on the Role of the Christian Family in the Modern World," number 11, at *www.vatican.va/holy_father/john_paul_ii/apost_exhortations/ documents/hf_jp-ii_exh_19811122_familiaris-consortio_en.html,* accessed January 31, 2005.

The excerpt on page 32 is from "Do 'Good People' Need Confession?: Self-Deception and the Sacrament of Honesty," by Edward Vacek, in *America,* February 25, 2002, page 13.

The excerpt on page 35 is from *Picture the Girl: Young Women Speak Their Minds,* by Audrey Shehyn (New York: Hyperion, 2000), page 66. Copyright © 2000 by Audrey Shehyn.

The excerpt on page 38 is from "The Science of Happiness," by Geoffrey Cowley, in *Newsweek,* September 2002, pages 46–47.

The story on page 42 is from *Every Step of the Way: Stories by Teenagers 4,* edited by Michael Wilt (Winona, MN: Saint Mary's Press, 1999), page 123. Copyright © 1999 by Saint Mary's Press. All rights reserved.

The excerpt on page 43 is from *Conjectures of a Guilty Bystander,* by Thomas Merton (Garden City, NY: Doubleday and Company, 1966), pages 140, 141, and 142. Copyright © 1965, 1966 by The Abbey of Gethsemani.

The three reflections on page 47 are adapted from *She Said . . . He Said: Teens Speak Out on Life and Faith,* edited by Laurie Delgatto (Winona, MN: Saint Mary's Press, 2003), pages 14, 10, and 12–13, respectively. Copyright © 2003 by Saint Mary's Press. All rights reserved.

The excerpt by Dorothy Day on page 53 is from *On Pilgrimage,* July to August, by Dorothy Day, Catholic Worker Movement, at *www.catholicworker.org/dorothyday/daytext.cfm?TextID=482,* accessed April 19, 2005.

The excerpt on page 55 is from *The Inner Voice of Love: A Journey Through Anguish to Freedom,* by Henri J. M. Nouwen (New York: Bantam Doubleday Dell Publishing Company, 1996), pages 80 and 81. Copyright © 1996 by Henri J. M. Nouwen.

The quotation by Pope Paul II on page 65 is from "Constitution on the Sacred Liturgy *Sacrosanctum Concilium* Solemnly Promulgated by His Holiness," at *www.vatican.va/archive/hist_councils/ii_vatican_council/documents/vatii_const_19631204_sacrosanctum-concilium_en.html,* accessed April 20, 2005.

The material in "Discerning Your Vocation" on page 74 is paraphrased from "Vocation Education," by James VanOosting, in *America,* July 1–July 8, 2002, pages 8–11.

The quotation by Catherine Bertrand on page 75 is from "On Responding to God's Call: Points to Consider," in *Origins,* February 15, 2001, volume 30, number 35, page 569.

The quotations on page 76 are from *Spiritual Quest: A Guide to the Changing Landscape,* by Thomas Hart (New York: Paulist Press, 1999), page 138. Copyright © 1999 by Thomas Hart.

The words of Mother Teresa on page 77 are from *My Life Serving the Poor,* by Mother Teresa, edited by José Luis González-Balado and Janet N. Playfoot (New York: Ballantine Books, 1985), page 2. Copyright © 1985 by José Luis González-Balado.

The words of Mother Teresa on page 78 are from *The Joy in Loving: A Guide to Daily Living with Mother Teresa,* compiled by Java Chaliha and Edward Le Joly (New York: Viking Penguin, 1997), page 145. Copyright © 1996 by Java Chaliha and Edward Le Joly.

The quotation on page 78 is from *The Saints' Guide to Happiness,* by Robert Ellsberg (New York: North Point Press, 2003), page 43. Copyright © 2003 by Robert Ellsberg.

The excerpt on page 79 is from *Wishful Thinking: A Theological ABC,* by Frederick Buechner (New York: Harper and Row, Publishers, 1973), page 95. Copyright © 1973 by Frederick Buechner.

The prayer on page 90 is from *Thoughts in Solitude,* by Thomas Merton (New York: Farrar, Straus and Giroux, 1956, 1958), page 83. Copyright © 1956, 1958 by The Abbey of Our Lady of Gethsemani. Copyright renewed 1986 by the Trustees of the Thomas Merton Legacy Trust. Reprinted by permission of Farrar, Straus and Giroux, LLC.

To view copyright terms and conditions for Internet materials cited here, log on to the home pages for the referenced Web sites.

During this book's preparation, all citations, facts, figures, names, addresses, telephone numbers, Internet URLs, and other pieces of information cited within were verified for accuracy. The authors and Saint Mary's Press staff have made every attempt to reference current and valid sources, but we cannot guarantee the content of any source, and we are not responsible for any changes that may have occurred since our verification. If you find an error in, or have a question or concern about, any of the information or sources listed within, please contact Saint Mary's Press.

Endnotes Cited in Quotations from the *Catechism of the Catholic Church*

Chapter 2

1. Cf. *Rev* 2:17.

Chapter 3

1. St. Augustine, *De morbis eccl.* 1, 3, 4: J. P. Migne, ed., Patrologia Latina (Paris: 1841–1855) 32, 1312.
2. *Lumen gentium* 11

Chapter 5

1. *Rom* 8:26.
2. *Eph* 5:19; St. Augustine, *En. in Ps.* 72, 1: J. P. Migne, ed., Patrologia Latina (Paris: 1841–1855) 36, 914; cf. *Col* 3:16.